The Truth Will Liberate You

CONTENTS

FOREWORD

There is probably no area of Christian thinking in which there are so many unproved theories, and in which so many unverified assertions are dragged in, as in the field of Christian freedom. Is it true that Paul did away with the law of Moses? What does the apostle mean when he says that the Christian is no longer under the law? Is it true that the new law gives you the strength to obey it? Is it an observable fact, or a mere assertion? Is it true that Judaism was a religion of the letter, while Christianity is a religion of the Spirit? Down through the ages, Catholic theology has bandied about a lot of slogans relating to the theme of Christian freedom. But can anyone confirm their truth by experience? Yet it is most certainly a fact that the first Christians felt that they were new men, and that they were free.

Therefore a return to the sources in this area is particularly desirable in order to avoid having the Christian existence become a schizophrenic double life and also to open a path to the openness and freedom of the gospel.

The material for the present study arose in several steps and on a number of levels: lecture material, discussion groups, the theme of a retreat. Through these the author arrived at the not particularly startling realization that his insights gained a new degree of clarity with each new approach, and that they came together with a new kind of cohesion each time. The obvious supposition is that this would happen again with the next approach, but one of the main ideas in this study is precisely that freedom consists in the acceptance of the genuine incompleteness, the radical openness, of human existence. That is why we entrust our thoughts to paper in full awareness that for many people this very incompleteness will constitute a jumping off point for new journeys into discovery. It is only in this way that this work can fulfill its task, which is to contribute something to **aggiornamento,** the updating of our Christianity.

"THE TRUTH WILL MAKE YOU FREE"

John 8:32

Anyone who wants to explore the question of the relation between freedom and law must first deal with the still more difficult question of what freedom itself is. For whoever wishes to be free, must first ask what he really wants. A difficult question, though at first sight it does not look difficult to answer. Freedom is in fact a basic human characteristic, one which distinguishes men from trees or animals. If I want to, I can abandon my typewriter and go take a vacation instead of writing this book. And yet, one of the greatest thinkers of our time asked himself quite earnestly if it were not contrary to the very nature of freedom to attempt to define it.[1] We are not concerned here about theory; this book has a purely practical aim. Over and above that, freedom is in the first place a matter of human experience rather than of theory. We all know perfectly well the feeling of relief that comes after a difficult examination—how you can wake up morning after morning, for weeks after the examination, with the feeling that a burden has been removed. We who belong to the middle-aged generation vividly remember the day of our country's liberation at the end of World War II, but everyone knows also that this feeling ebbs rapidly, its place being taken by new cares and new worries. Experience also teaches that the celebrations of our liberation don't last very long—that they can be kept up only with a dose of artificial prodding. And over and above this, being free is something very different from being freed. Knowing how to liberate oneself is nothing; to be able to be free, that is the difficult thing (André Gide).[2] But it is extremely difficult to define what being free actually is. One can specify much more closely what it means to free oneself, or to be freed, because one can do that in terms of that from which he is liberated. We can be free from sickness, free from work, from war, and so on. But when all these things are gone, am I then free? The freedom which remains is endless boredom, freedom from nothingness; and that is death. This is the conclusion to which the French philosopher Sartre comes: "I am free, I no longer have any reason to live; all the tried and true reasons have fallen away, and I cannot think up any new ones. I'm still young enough, I have strength enough to begin all over again. But where should I start? . . . I'm alone in this white street, gardens in front of every house. Alone and free. But this freedom is rather like death."[3] Indeed, when I have liberated myself from everything, there is only one thing left for me, and that is to free myself from life, so as to escape from boredom and revulsion. But is it really possible for me to dispose of my own life freely? As Paul says: "For no one of us lives, and equally no one of us dies, for

himself alone" (Rom. 14:7, av). We are going to have
to return to this question, but in any case it is already
evident that we are not going to be able to define our
understanding of freedom by following this course,
because this reasoning arrives at nothing, at death.

Human freedom is, in fact, not absolute. Actually,
it is a certain freedom of choice. I am able to choose
from among a certain number of possibilities, but
these possibilities are given in advance, and they are
not unlimited. Moreover, chosing means a new limitation, because when I choose one alternative, I rule
out all the others. Thus, my freedom is limited in
two ways: in the first place it is related to the
circumstances in which I find myself, so that the
number of choices is limited, but more than that,
because of the relativity of the human condition itself
it is impossible to have everything all at the same
time, so that from among these limited possibilities,
I can select only one. To use the terms of Thomistic
philosophy, we are an **esse ab alio.** Our existence
does not come forth out of ourselves, but out of
Another. We receive it from the hand of God, who
also measures out the dimensions of our existence.
And God calls us into existence by the mediation of
our fellow men. The fact that we exist is something
of which we are aware only because other men also
exist, and because things exist, so in this sense, too,
our existence is dependent upon others.

Sartre says, "I am alone and free," but he would
not be able to say that if he were really alone. We
are able to know that we are free only because there

are other people who are able to infringe our freedom.[4] The state of human existence is an existence-
in-the-world, an existence-among-men, or, as modern
philosophy puts it, to exist is to coexist.[5] Now, if this
is true, I must achieve my freedom jointly with my
fellow man. My freedom must not make unfreedom
for someone else. If it were otherwise, there could
be only one free man in the world, and he would be a
tyrant with everyone else under his thumb. And as a
matter of fact, that person would not be free either.
No, he would be the least free man in existence,
because he could not take a single step without feeling
threatened on every side. Those who suppress others
are not themselves free, Karl Marx is reported to have
said. I am human to the extent that I allow others
to be human, only as free as I let other men be. I
experience the fact that I am a person, that I am an
"I," to the extent that I affirm the reality of the other
person's "thou," and to the extent that I accept his
being different. That is why the hermit who has no
contact with other men is no freer than the tyrant.

Moreover, that hermit (and this is a new point of
view) can also become a slave to himself, to his own
ideas and moods. So, in this sense a man is never
alone. He always brings himself along with him. It
happens so often that a person, finding himself in
a certain situation, job, place of abode, or whatever,
flees from it because he wants to be free, and then,
within a short time comes to the realization that in
his new circumstances he experiences the very same
difficulties over again. No one can be liberated from

himself, nobody can be free from his own shadow. That's why the Greek philosophers, or at least a certain school of them, teach that a man becomes free by learning to control his unruly desires and by giving up his unattainable dreams. So we see that to be free is not to be free from something, it is to be free for something: the possibility of developing in oneself true humanity, the ability to become an "ideal" person. We find this same concept of freedom recurring in the philosophers of the seventeenth and eighteenth centuries: freedom is not being able to do what you want to do, it is the ability to want to be what you have to be. Modern philosophy has complemented and corrected this concept in the light of the fact that to be human is always a state of being among men, and a state of being within this world. Thus it can be realized only within the boundaries that are set for us by these circumstances. Our freedom is a situational freedom—for me, a coming to terms with the situation in which I am placed. Why do I have the feeling that I am free when I am in the open countryside? If there is one place I am not free, it is there, where everything that surrounds me is just as it is, and I cannot change it in any way. But I am aware that it has to be as it is, I accept that, and so I am free. On the other hand, suppose I am a bird fancier and I have an aviary, then the fact that there are birds flying about at liberty is something that interferes with my freedom. I am not content with the fact that there are birds flying about. I want to have those birds. The window that bangs because my careless neighbor neglected to fasten it irritates me and interferes with my work. The train that rattles by at regular intervals does not bother me, because I know the train cannot help being there.

Human freedom can blossom only amid the objectivity of life's given facts, which a person can tie up together into a harmonious whole by ordering and understanding them in a satisfying way. There are certain rules which spring up spontaneously in this game of togetherness, rules which make living together possible. We call these rules "the natural law." This law is not imposed upon us from without, but is the "natural" consequence of human dependency, and this dependent condition is the very essence of humanity which, as we have already said, is always an existence-among-men. As a result, law is not a hindrance to freedom but, rather, it serves freedom. It should be put even more strongly than that: human freedom is necessarily dependent on laws, because the existence of man is itself dependent.

This is a principle which might be called Christian without further qualification. St. Paul does not mean anything else when he says: "My brothers, you were called, as you know, to liberty; but be careful, or this liberty will provide an opening for self-indulgence. Serve one another, rather, in works of love, since the whole of the Law is summarized in a single commandment: Love your neighbor as yourself" (Gal. 5:13-14). So, then, freedom is an ideal to which we are called, not something that falls into our laps like ripe fruit. Moreover, this quotation makes it clear to what dangers human freedom is exposed. In the first place, the ideal can be blotted out by human self-seeking, by what is called "the flesh." That is the word the apostle uses. Even though I come to understand that true freedom consists in genuine humanity, that does not mean that I am necessarily going to be willing and able to realize the ideal. The great fault of Greek thought was that it quite simply equated freedom in the mind with freedom in action. This shows up in a peculiar way in the translation of the Old Testament. In the Septuagint—that is, the Greek translation of the Old Testament—the idea of conversion, which in Hebrew means a complete re-orientation of the entire person and therefore is a moral concept, is translated by the Greek word **metanoia,** which simply means changing one's mind or manner of thinking. St. Paul's experience is that, following my inner being, I take pleasure in God's law, but in my deeds I have to recognize that there is another law which works against "the law which my reason dictates" (Rom. 7:23). There is no doubt that an ideal may exude an appealing strength, but there is also a strong force which wars against it, and the fact is that nobody is as good, and, fortunately, nobody is quite as bad, as the teaching which he advocates. Experience teaches that man is able to act without reason, even against reason, that he will violate his own existence and destroy himself. There are many cases in which freedom means nothing more than pretending after the fact that I might have done otherwise. While the decision was still in front of us, the role played by judgment was usually much smaller than we imagine afterward.

The philosophy of past ages also suffered from an unbridled optimism. During the stormy course of the development of natural science, man's knowledge of himself grew to such an extent that he came to believe that the submission of the whole earth to him was only a matter of time. But in fact man has become the slave of his own discoveries. The threat of atomic destruction presses down on our age like a leaden weight, and no matter how often we are assured that people are getting wiser and wiser, experience teaches us that man has never discovered anything without sooner or later succumbing to the temptation to misuse his discovery. Hence the feverish search for counterweapons and protective measures. It is the aim of all inventions to make life easier, and consequently to make man increasingly free. But when, for example, advances in automation threaten to cause large-scale unemployment, we find ourselves unable to arrest the process.[6] There is a relation between this and the development of modern concepts of freedom. The freethinkers who sought to liberate themselves from religious and ecclesiastical traditions were imbued with the optimistic supposition that basically everybody thinks in the same way, and that it is possible to construct an orderly society on the foundation of this universal belief. As long as their thinking continued to be guided unconsciously by the inheritance of more than a thousand years of Christian tradition, it continued to look as if this ideal could indeed be fulfilled. However, the last half century has taught us to what a pretty pass mankind can come when the profound relationship between freedom and interdependence is forgotten, and man tries to be totally autonomous. Then he is driven willy-nilly to the conclusion: either God exists but I do not exist or I exist but God does not exist (Sartre).[7] And with this he falls at once into the primal sin of Eden, the refusal to care for God's garden, the refusal to work His royal domains like an indentured servant. By this refusal man destroys his freedom, and the longing to be free becomes a **passion inutile.** The myth of Sisyphus, who keeps trying to roll the boulder back up the mountain, is the classic expression of man's absurd instinct for infinitude, man, who because he can never reach the goal of absolute freedom, lives under the doom of a passion for an unattainable goal of the heart. Sartre says we are doomed to be free,[8] and the meaning of hell consists for him in the presence of others whose existence prevents us from being absolutely free.[9]

Just at the point where the Greek and humanist ideal of freedom butts its head against the stone wall of human interdependence, the Christian ideal of acceptance takes over. Man must always be choosing between revolution and resignation (Sartre), but this resignation is not necessarily tied up with inner rebelliousness. It can also be a loving acceptance, and then it becomes freedom. This is the way that St. Paul shows us in the Letter to the Galatians quoted above. The call to freedom is present in every man, and this basic human longing leads either to self-seeking, or it finds satisfaction in loving service. But man does not discover this way by his own strength.

A French proverb says: "Aimer c'est décentraliser." Whoever wants to love has to turn his back on himself, and turn himself toward God and his fellow man. This is something we are unable to do of ourselves. By his own nature a man revolves about his own axis. Left to himself, he describes smaller and smaller circles about his own center, until finally he falls all over himself. At that point the better self, the knowledge that guides our action—con-scientia—becomes identical with our natural inclinations, so that the better has been absorbed completely by the worse. Therefore, a power outside ourselves is necessary, and this power is called love. It is only when we get into the field of its attraction that we are, so to speak, in a magnetic field that can pull us out of our egocentricity. When this happens, a person reaches a state of equilibrium between the absolute autonomy of the un-man and the utter dependency of the beast. Perhaps we can compare this state to the weightlessness of the astronaut, who is away from the gravitational field of the earth, but who keeps within the orbit of his precisely calculated course. A person is part of the world, but at the same time he can set himself over against the world, to master and subdue it. In the story of creation, we are told that God made woman out of man to be a helper to complement him. Thus every man has his fellow man to thank for his origin and for his status. This is obviously true in the biological sense, but even more importantly because it is other people who make him truly a person. And at the same time a man can put himself in opposition to mankind, and he can freely love or hate mankind, because he is an independent being, a person. Growth into true humanity takes place by means of this balancing of freedom and constraint. The choice is always before a man, either to make his own life, which results in his losing his true humanity or, on the other hand, losing himself to the other person, and thereby finding himself (Matt. 10:39).

The Bible clearly expresses the fact that our egoism does not merely prevent us from doing the truth, but it also blinds us so that we cannot even see the truth (John 3:21; 1 John 1:6). The biblical word for "law" is **torah**, a word which really means "indication." In Joshua 18:6 we read that Joshua casts lots (**jarah**) to find out how the land of Canaan is to be divided up, and this Godly indication is to be law, **torah** for all time. The quotation from John 8:32 which heads this chapter is words which Jesus spoke to Jews who were convinced that they were free. "We are descended from Abraham and we have never been the slaves of anyone." So it looks as if anybody can be a slave, even if he is perfectly sure he is free. We said previously that freedom consists in willing what has to be. The trouble is that we do not actually know just what it is we have to be, we do not really know in what true humanity consists. What freedom really is harks back to the question of what humanity really is, the problem of what it is to be a man. A man looking for freedom is a little like a dog trying to catch his tail. It's not just strength from outside that we need in order to become

free, we also need a source of light to illuminate
our way:

> Now your word is a lamp to my feet,
>   a light on my path.
> I have sworn to observe, I shall maintain,
>   your righteous rulings. . . .
> As your word unfolds, it gives light,
>   and the simple understand.
> I open my mouth, panting
>   eagerly for your commandments.
>   Psalm 119:105-106, 130-131

For this reason we start our reflection about the relationship between freedom and law from the Bible;
it is there primarily that we find the truth which
shall make us free. "If you make my word your
home," Christ says, "you will indeed be my disciples"
(John 8:31), and He follows this by saying: "so if the
son makes you free, you will be free indeed" (John
8:36). Now, the initial results of our search for this
truth are rather disappointing. Our natural human
inclination is to look first for what the Bible has to
say about freedom. It seems that in the entire Old
Testament the word "freedom" appears only once,
in Leviticus 19:20, and in this case it means to be
freed from slavery. The stem of this word appears in
other places, but still always in connection with
slavery.[10] Does this mean that the longing for freedom
had not yet been awakened in the people of Israel?
No one who follows the history of Israel from that
day to this could possibly come to that conclusion.
But then how is the remarkable absence of this
elementary human concept to be explained?

Perhaps this fact is due to another linguistic phenomenon, which might at first sight seem to have nothing to do with it. As far as we can discover by research, the Bible is the only place in the whole of legal writing where law is called the Word, without any further qualification. We could drag out any number of proof texts for this statement, but there is one which will suffice to represent them all at this point, the very well-known Deuteronomy 30:11-14, to which we will soon be returning in another connection:

"For this Law that I enjoin on you today is not beyond your strength or beyond your reach. It is not in heaven, so that you need to wonder 'Who will go up to heaven for us and bring it down to us, so that we may hear it and keep it?' Nor is it beyond the seas, so that you need to wonder, 'Who will cross the seas for us and bring it back to us, so that we may hear and keep it?' No, the Word is very near to you, it is in your mouth and in your heart for your observance."

Is it not possible that the man of the Bible, did not think of the law as an impediment to freedom, because, as far as he was concerned, the law was the Word? And God's Word possesses a creative power:

By the word of Yahweh the heavens were made,
their whole array by the breath of his mouth;
he collects the ocean waters as though in a
    wineskin,
he stores the deeps in cellars.

> Let the whole world fear Yahweh,
> let all who live on earth revere him!
> he spoke and it was created;
> he commanded, and there it stood.
>
> Psalm 33:6-9

In these words from the Psalms there is already a suggestion, spelled out expressly elsewhere, that there is a connection between the Word of Creation and the law:

> He gives an order;
> his word flashes to earth:
> to spread snow like a blanket,
> to strew hoarfrost like ashes, . . .
>
> Psalm 147:15-16

> He reveals his word to Jacob,
> his statutes and rulings to Israel:
> he never does this for other nations,
> he never reveals his rulings to them.
>
> Psalm 147:19-20

There is a close relation between these two explanations of the term "the Word of God," first as the deed of creation, and second as the law. God has created man, and has at the same time limited him in his existence. Likewise, the law sets boundaries for man, but these serve to lead man's life into fixed paths, and so to make him into a genuine man. With respect to the powers of nature, man feels himself to be dependent and vulnerable. In the light of God's law he learns to understand himself as a human being, that is to say, as a limited and dependent creature. So, too, God's law is light and darkness at one and the same time. It teaches man what he has to do, but at the same time it hides from him why he has

to do it (Deut. 29:28). "Things hidden belong to
Yahweh our God, but things revealed are ours and
our children's for all time, so that we may observe
all the words of this Law." The relations between
these two things lies principally in the fact that the
law of God shares in the power of His creative omnipotence, and completes the work of His hands.[11] "Take
all these words to heart; I call them to witness against
you today. You must order your children to keep
and observe all the words of this Law. It is no idle
thing you will be doing, for the Law is your life"
(Deut. 32:46-47). It occurs to me that this is precisely
the explanation of why Israel experienced servitude
to the law of God as freedom. The law is God's
Word, which touches man in his relativity from out
of the infinite, and which awakens in him a homesickness for the Absolute. This call is capable of
liberating him from bondage to his own "freedom,"
and to raise him up to the unknown heights of
nearness to God. This book intends to be a modest
effort to translate God's Word into the language of
modern self-interpretation. It cannot be anything
more than an attempt, a reaching out in the right
direction. But the philosophy of language teaches us
that men's words are always outdoing themselves,
and that they can conjure up in others more than the
person who uttered them actually knew himself.

2

"AND YAHWEH SPOKE
TO MOSES"

LEVITICUS 1:1, AV

The law of the Old Testament is known as the
Mosaic law, or the law of Moses (Luke 22:44; John
1:17; 7:19-23; 8:5; Acts 28:23, 38, etc.). This familiar
expression hides an interesting phenomenon, for, even
if one joins with those many serious scholars who
believe that the heart of the Book of Laws, the Ten
Commandments, Exodus 20:1-17, and the so-called
Book of the Covenant (Exod. 20:22-23: 19) are at least
in their broad outline the work of Moses, there still
remains an enormous amount of law of which this
cannot be said, and which is quite evidently of later
origin. A great deal of this legislation ·presupposes
that Israel lives in cities and is engaged in agriculture,
which makes it unreasonable to suppose that the
laws come from the time in which Israel still led a
nomadic life. Even in the central portion which we
have just mentioned there are emendations which
stem from a later time. For example, we read in the
law of the Sabbath, in the Third Commandment,
"You shall do no work that day, neither you nor your
son nor your daughter nor your servants, men or
women, nor your animals nor the stranger who lives
with you" (Exod. 20:10). Also in the Book of the

Covenant it speaks of houses, no longer of tents as in Exodus 22:7, which points to the settled life.

We cannot elaborate on this matter here. Anyone who thinks these indications, which are intended only as an illustration, are not sufficient is urged to read an introduction to the Pentateuch, in which he will discover that currently people believe the so-called books of Moses were written between 850 and 400 B.C.[1] A far more important question for us is where the tendency to put all laws into the gray past came from. After all, this is not limited to the Bible; it is a human tendency everywhere. It is true of every people that their laws derive authority from their antiquity. "It has always been that way" is an argument we spontaneously fall back on to point up the reasonableness of a law, and when we are face to face with an important decision of conscience, we instinctively look for a similar situation in the past, hoping to find something with which we can conform.

May this tendency not perhaps come from the fact that people are aware of the truth that laws really do have a pre-existence? When someone formulates a law, he does not create it out of nothing, he merely gives shape to something formless and unknown which already lives within him. To put it differently, he "translates" the eternal law of God into the language of his own time and situation. In the beautiful hymn to Wisdom in the Book of Sirach (chapter 24), the praises of the eternal procession of the divine Wisdom are sung, but, as the last verses

make quite clear, this Wisdom is nothing other than
the law of Moses:

> I came forth from the mouth of the Most High,
>   and I covered the earth like mist.
> I had my tent in the heights,
>   and my throne in a pillar of cloud. . . .
> From eternity, in the beginning, he created me
>   and for eternity I shall remain.
> I ministered before him in the holy tabernacle,
>   and thus was I established in Zion.
> All this is no other than the book of the
>   covenant of the Most High God,
>   the Law that Moses enjoined on us.
>   Sirach 24:3-4, 10-11, 23-24

In the Midrash, the Jewish commentary on the
law, the law itself has become a pre-existent divine
being which was God's counselor at the creation of
the world.[2] The prologue to the Fourth Gospel is also
strongly reminiscent of all this. It sings of the eternal
procession of the Word of God:

> In the beginning was the Word;
> the Word was with God
> and the Word was God.
> He was with God in the beginning.
> Through him all things came to be,
> not one thing had its being but through him.
>   John 1:1-3

As a matter of fact, there seems to be a literary
relationship between St. John's Prologue and the
Hymn to Wisdom in the Book of Sirach. But what
is even more important is that there is a correspondence in content, because, as we have just said, if each
law is a manifestation of the eternal law of God, then

this is only a special case of a universal principle. To one degree or another it could be said of every word of man that it is "a reflection of the eternal light, untarnished mirror of God's active power, image of his goodness" (Wisd. 7:26). From the very moment when humankind first took up the Word, and the process of becoming human was an actuality, a divine seed began to grow in man, as 1 John 3:9 tells us. Through the ages this human word became ever riper and deeper in content, laden with wisdom and experience of God, generation by generation, so that man's heart was prepared in the fullness of time (Gal. 4:4; Eph. 1:10) to receive the hypostatic divine Word. We shall return in greater detail to this matter of the God-laden character of the human word, as well as of human law. At this point it is sufficient to remark that, like every word of man, every law has had a pre-existence, and that man's inclination to project laws into the past finds its explanation as well as its rationale there.

Actually, what is even more disquieting to the inexperienced reader than the antedating of the law is the fact that the Bible seems to say that the whole law was dictated to Moses by God himself. The quotation which heads this chapter recurs like a refrain, ten times over, in Leviticus.

The degrees of the marital relationship, directions for the later harvest, in short, all of life down to its smallest detail is regulated by God. When the Orthodox Jew of today goes about wearing curly sideburns, he does it in literal obedience to Leviticus 19:28, which forbids idolatrous practices that were current among neighboring peoples. "You are not to round off your hair at the edges nor trim the edges of your beard. You are not to gash your bodies when some-one dies, and you are not to tattoo yourselves. I am Yahweh" (Lev. 19:28-29). This refrain "I am Yahweh" returns again and again. The problem becomes more difficult when we learn that many of these laws have parallels in the old compendia of laws of other Near Eastern peoples, such as the Hittites, Assyrians, and Egyptians—which is not to say that the law of Israel lacks original characteristics. For example, the king does not act as the lawgiver, but insofar as he is named in the law (and as a matter of fact he is not often named), he is subject to the law. This is unique in the ancient Near East, and is quite different from the provisions of the laws of other nations. The con-nection between the law and the Covenant set forth in Deuteronomy 17:14-20 has no parallel in the writ-ings of the surrounding peoples. But this does not change the fact that parallels to nearly the whole of the civil law of Israel can be found in such old law books as the great Code of Hammurabi of Babylon (ca. 1700 b.c.). As a matter of fact it is even true that certain of Israel's laws are entirely incomprehensible without referring to that literature. For example, no one really understood what was meant by Exodus 23:19; 34:26, or Deuteronomy 14:21: "You are not to boil a kid in its mother's milk." This did not become clear until about 1930, when the writings of ancient Ugarit were excavated, in which it was made plain that the boiling of a kid in its mother's milk was a special kind of sacrifice which evidently was carried out in several places in the land of Canaan. For the same reason, the offering of honey was forbidden in Leviticus 2:11.[3] As if these problems weren't already intriguing enough, the stone stele on which the Code of Hammurabi was chiseled, and which is now in the Louvre, is surmounted by an image of the king who is depicted as receiving the book of the Law from the hand of the Sun god, the judge of heaven. Yet this must not be taken to indicate that Israel merely borrowed its laws outright from the legislation of neighboring peoples. It is, rather, that the similarities must be explained by the fact there existed a widespread common law and custom upon which all the codes of the peoples of the ancient Near East were based.[4] The very way in which they are phrased shows us that the greater proportion of Israel's law stems from these customs. In truth, there are two quite distinct kinds of law in the law of Moses. First, there are the so-called apodictic laws, which are introduced by the phrase, "Thou shalt" ("You must"). These seem to be the laws that are of Israelite origin. Side by side with these are the casuistic laws, which are introduced by the words, "If someone shall." The form of words clearly indicates that these spring from jurisprudence, and most of such laws have parallels in other Near Eastern formularies. A single illustration will suffice, from Exodus 21:2-6:

> When you buy a Hebrew slave, his service shall be for six years. In the seventh year he may leave; he shall be free, with no compensation to pay. If he came single, he shall leave single;

if he came married, his wife shall leave with him. If his master gives him a wife and she bears him sons and daughters, wife and children shall belong to her master, and the man must leave alone. But if the slave declares, "I love my master and my wife and children; I renounce my freedom," then his master shall take him to God, leading him to the door or the door post. His master shall pierce his ear with an awl, and he shall be in his service for all time.

It should be remarked that this law from the Book of the Covenant also dates from a later time, even though "door post" could be translated as "tent pole."[5]

It must be quite obvious by now that all these laws could not possibly have been literally dictated to Moses. They must have originated from the decisions of judges. In other words, the divine origin of the laws of the Old Testament is a literary device. We must examine its meaning more closely. We can see the emergence of this literary convention in the Bible itself. As religious development progressed in Israel, it was felt necessary to put a greater distance between God and man, so as to stress more strongly the transcendence of God. The picture of God writing the law with His own finger would not fit into this later view (Exod. 24:12; 31:18; 32:16; Deut. 9:10). Thus, in the later passages this picture is restricted to the Ten Commandments, the core of the law (Exod. 34:28-Deut. 4:13; 5:22; 10:4). Moses becomes the mediator who issues laws in the name of God (Deut. 4:44, **vide** Gal. 3:19; Acts 7:38), and the law acquires the name "law of Moses" (Josh. 8:31; 2 Kings 14:6;

2 Chron. 25:4; Neh. 13:1). In still later passages, Moses receives the law not directly from the hand of God but by the mediation of angels (Deut. 33:2, in the Greek translation; Acts 7:38, 53; Gal. 3:19; Heb. 2:2). The Bible is outlining a process of development here, and if we follow the line further along, we have the idea that the law has come out of the experience of men living together in society, and that the story of stone tablets is a literary figure which clothes the deepest truth in simple words.

Even more important than this conclusion is the question of what deeper truth it is that is signified here. Our obedience to the law hinges on our answer to the question, By what right have the Bible and the Church clothed human laws with divine authority? The starting point for an investigation into what we may call the transcendence of the law is the universal conviction that there exists a norm of behavior which is independent of us. This conviction is so strong that when a person makes a rule for himself alone—for example, he determines to give up smoking—he externalizes the rule, and begins a dialogue with himself: "In this case it is very hard to refuse to light up." The French novelist Simenon, who is noted for his fine psychological portraits, has a noteworthy description of this tendency. The protagonist of his novel **The Man with a Dog,** written in the first person, has to endure a long term in prison. He feels so happy during this time that the prison doctor, wondering if he is not mentally disturbed, advises him to be examined by a neurologist. Looking back on it later,

he comes to the conclusion that he is still living in a
prison anyway, except that the one he usually lives in
is bigger, and bounded by certain streets instead of
walls. "I pay great heed to the rules I have set for
myself, or have accepted, and thus I remain ringed
about by invisible walls." While still in prison he had
already come to this insight: "Have not monks for
many ages been choosing a kind of life that is very
nearly the same as this? And how many people who
live in the middle of a city submit themselves to a
vast number of habits and rules, which are really
more confining than those of a prison?"[6] Anyone who
has had experience with the life of monks, or who,
being a monk, has any degree of self-knowledge,
knows how easy it is for this self-imposed and self-
chosen rule to appear to have been imposed from
outside, so that the monk is always trying to get
round it, to haggle and come to terms with it.

Where, then, does this remarkable tendency of
people always to look for a norm outside themselves
come from? And to do this even when it is really a
question of a rule one had made for himself? Does it
not come from the fact that men instinctively feel
they have to protect themselves from themselves; that
what we ordinarily call freedom is in fact slavery to
the whims and impulses of the moment? Genuine
freedom consists in being free from that particular
kind of freedom. But this is possible only when our
actions are regulated by a motif that stands apart
from momentary impressions; which is the same as
saying transcendental laws.[7]

True freedom, then, does not consist in avoiding being tied down, but in being attentive to a law in which one recognizes the meaning of his existence. Or, paradoxically, the measure of our freedom is in the degree of our obedience to the law of our life. Freedom is not a sort of autonomy, not being a law unto oneself. On the other hand, obedience to the law should not be regarded as a kind of heteronomy, as contrasted with autonomy. That is, it is not submission to a foreign law or set of laws, because law ultimately springs from the soul of mankind itself and, therefore, the most truly autonomous person is the one who is the most engaged in things, just as Gabriel Marcel says in **Etre et Avoir**.[8] He uses the example of the artist, the difference between talent and genius, to demonstrate this. A real artist, that is to say, a genius, cannot summon up his inspiration. He must wait for a hallowed moment, and when he has been seized by it, he throws himself into his work to such an extent that he scarcely has time to eat or sleep. The craftsman, on the other hand—the person who has talent—calmly puts his work down in the evening, and takes it up again the following morning. The craftsman is exercising his skill; the artist is possessed by his. Even linguistic usage shows this, for we say that someone **has** talent, but someone **is** a genius. And yet, everyone will admit that the artist lives in greater freedom than the merely talented person, just as the philosopher is freer than the scientist, and the holy man more free than the merely virtuous one. Marcel tells us that this occurs because the artist's lack of autonomy is not really heteronomy, just as love is not heterocentric. The person who truly loves revolves with his whole being round the object of his love. But it is, and it remains his love, finding its source inalienably on this side of the self. Hence the lack of autonomy which is involved is itself freedom, and there is no person freer than the one who is in love.

So when Israel acknowledges the law which it has itself shaped to be the law of the Highest, this does not mean that it is adoring the work of its own hands, because its own plan for life really is the expression for its own time of God's eternal will. The imagery of God engraving the law on stone tablets with His own finger is the primitive expression of the awareness that man, when he creates a' law for life, outdoes himself, and participates in the creative acts of God.

This manifestation is not unique; it is a particularization of that self-surpassing quality which is characteristic of the human word in general. We human beings bring other people to the state of being human by the speaking of words. Whenever a mother calls her child by name and speaks endearing words to it, she calls it out of the night of unconsciousness into genuine humanity. Were she to fail to do this, the child would remain immature and vacuous. This has been shown in numerous experiments by psychologists, and their findings are confirmed by the existence of the "hospital syndrome," that illness of children who for one reason or another have grown up in an institution. But, to tell the truth, we don't require the

experiments of the psychologist to know this. Everyone engaged in pastoral work knows from his own
experience the tragic cases of people who have never
become fully human because they have never been
spoken to, because they have never had the opportunity to hear words that said something to them,
words that did something to them. The word, Heideg-
ger tells us, is **das Haus des Seins,** the house, or home,
of being; and when a child asks his parents, "What
is that called?" he is in effect asking them to give
him a share in their humanity. Therefore, whenever
people truly speak (for it must be admitted also that
there is such a thing as an idle word, one that is
empty and accomplishes nothing; Matt. 12:36), they
take part in the creative omnipotence of God. To
speak a word is to exceed oneself, much as people
exceed themselves in procreation, and bring into being
not merely an organism, but a person; one who can
love and hate independently of them. In speaking,
then, a person shares in the power of the eternal
Word, "through whom all things came to be" (John
1:3). The Bible teaches us that in the beginning God
created everything by the Word of His power, but
science tells us that in fact the world came into
being by means of a process of development which
is still going on, and by means of which the laws
God had infused into His creation from the very beginning emerged and evolved simultaneously through
the work of mankind. It is in a similar fashion that
we must understand the Bible when it teaches us that
God gave man a complete book of laws. This is the
primitive way of expressing the fact that God infused

into man the power to discover himself and to develop in the direction which God established from the beginning.

As we have said before, the Jewish people were the first in the history of the relationship between God and man to identify law with the Word of God. They were also the first to seek freedom in a correspondence between human will and God's plan. These insights were the inexhaustible wellspring of religious inspiration for Israel down through the ages. "Israel, blessed are we: / what pleases God has been revealed to us" (Bar. 4:4). But, at the same time the germ of a later misfortune lies here. Because, as soon as the word is spoken it acquires substance, and begins to lead an independent existence, cut off from the person who utters it. It then acquires a fixed value which makes intersubjectivity, that is the conversation of men with one another, possible. But, at the same time, it loses thereby its connection with the living spirit which called it into life, and it becomes a dead letter (2 Cor. 3:6). Then when this same word is put down in writing, the risk of petrification takes a deadly shape. So we see how in Israel the picture of God giving the law with His own hand resulted in the image of a book which came down ready-made out of the sky, as is also said of the Koran (Ezek. 2:9; Zech. 5:1-4). We need scarcely add that this was a dangerous development for the law. The law of nature which had come forth from the living heart of man drifted farther and farther away from the source of its nourishment, and became petrified into a hard, lifeless set of rules.

As we have said before, the word continually sur-
passes the person who utters it, and it has results
which exceed its human power. But there is a con-
verse which is also true. Our thoughts are always
loftier than our words, and no single word can
represent precisely what we think and feel. This
holds true even more strongly when the human word
we are dealing with is the expression of the mind of
God. Fundamentally, every word is always a fore-
word; the Word of God most of all. So the law can
never be anything more than a provisional reflection
of God's eternal plan for mankind. The law is bound
up with a certain age, and can therefore never fully
encompass the eternal. It must always remain open to
further refinement. The word of the law must therefore be eschatological, that is to say, it must be
directed toward the end time, which alone can bring
us the completion of revelation.

The first thing this requires of the human lawgiver is a deep humility, stemming from a realization
of his own limitations and contingency. Only the
person who is totally free from bondage to his own
loves and his own pride is in fit condition to summon
up this openness to the future. He has to learn that
each day has enough worries of its own (Matt. 6:34),
because the person who is forever worrying about the
future is just as dead as the one who cannot break
away from the past. At the same time, he must have
a deep trust in the human beings who are going to
come after him. Whenever mankind tries to make
"eternal" laws, it is an expression of unbounded

arrogance. No one of us can have the last word. Those who come after us will know better, and they will be able to express it better than we.

Man's word can be maintained thanks to the continuous tension between a static or inertial element and a dynamic element, the factor of growth. It is a wonderful fact that we can continually say new things with the oldest of words. Great poets have seldom used neologisms, have seldom coined new words for themselves. When modern art tries to express itself in totally new and odd forms it may merely be evidencing its impotence. Old words are rich in warmth and wisdom which they have won from the thought and love of generation upon generation. Art consists of the ability of man to "bring out from his storeroom things both new and old" (Matt. 13:52), to capture what has never been said before in words which carry the patina of the ages.

Lawgiving, too, is conditioned by the tension between these two elements, the static and the dynamic. When the static element gains the upper hand, it leads to petrification and legalism. If, on the other hand, the element of growth becomes predominant, the result is often lawlessness, because a failure in the stability of law leads inevitably to a loss of respect for the law. Legalism and lawlessness, however contradictory they may sound, come ultimately from the same fundamental defect in human nature— a lack of self-surrender and trust. The person who cannot comply with the law, and the person who wants to set everything down rigidly in black and

white are equally prideful. Neither has any trust in
his fellow man. For reliance and trust are not
ultimately defined by their object, they are possibilities which lie within man himself, and consist principally of the ability to get outside oneself and
forget oneself. When Christ says that the first and
second commandments are one, it is not fundamentally because He wants to assert that God and man
are one, but because the love of God demands of us
the same surrender as does the love of our fellow
man. What He says about love is equally valid for
trust, which is but love with a particular coloration.
Faith, hope, and love—these three remain always
(1 Cor. 13:13).

The continual tension between the two elements
is also evident in the history of religion, because
human pride is always playing a role. The static
element in Israel, and as a matter of fact in all
religions, is represented by the priests who, by virtue
of their office, are the upholders of law and order.
The dynamic element is embodied in the prophets,
who are the bearers of the spirit which blows where
it will (John 3:5). This distinction naturally is rather
global. Even in the priestly caste there were prophets,
Ezekiel for example. On the other hand, every sanc-
tuary had professional "prophets" attached to it. But
in broad outline it is possible to say that the fortunes
of the Jewish religion were dominated by the continual tension between the letter and the spirit. In
the chapter which follows, we shall try to throw
some light on one of the facets of this tension.

3

"YOU . . . BUILD THE SEPULCHRES
OF THE PROPHETS"

MATTHEW 23:29

We are familiar with the concept that a prophet is someone who can foresee the future. A prophet who eats bread (Amos. 7:12) is a prophet whose predictions do not come true. This is a description which coincides only partially with biblical truth. According to Deuteronomy 34:10, Moses is the greatest of all the prophets, but one will have a hard time finding any predictions attributed to him. The Fathers found a way out of this. They told us that Moses had seen the whole history of the future in a sort of flashback. When he wrote about the creation of the world in Genesis, he was practicing prophecy in retrospect. Actually, this is not as foolish an idea as it may sound, because the writer of Genesis is working with the same kind of material as the prophets who foretold the messianic era. But, no matter how ingenious the solution may be, the truth lies elsewhere. The Greek word **prophetes** does indeed mean "fore-sayer," but in fact he is not a person who tells us about the future ahead of time; he is someone who speaks on behalf of someone else. He is therefore the mouthpiece of God: "They have left for Egypt without consulting me," God accuses the Jews who have not listened to the prophet (Isa. 30:2); and to Jeremiah he says: "If you utter noble, not despicable thoughts, you shall be as my own mouth" (Jer. 15:19).

Thus, in common speech he is called the "man of God," a man who in thought and deed and desire is so very much one with God that we hear the Word of God in him. Jesus of Nazareth, too, must have given His contemporaries the impression that He was a "man of God." He was not instantly recognized to be the royal personage, the Messiah, nor even the high priest of the New Covenant, but people nonetheless saw in him someone who was driven by the "Spirit." The most anyone could pretend was that it was an evil spirit, and they did that, too (Matt. 12:24). But even his bitterest enemies could not deny that he was driven by a higher power. Currently much is said about the pro-existence of Christ and by this is meant that His whole existence was a being-for-men. But He was pro-existent in a much more profound sense. It was His mission to give form to the being-for-men of God himself, to make this visible for us. Thus He exists "for" God as the prophet speaks for God, that is to say: in the place of God. His contemporaries sensed this quite well: "A great prophet has appeared among us; God has visited his people" (Luke 7:16).

How, then, do we explain the fact that the prophets kept themselves so busy with visions of the future that this came to be thought of as their characteristic occupation? The solution of this riddle, like that of many other riddles with which the Bible faces us, lies in the fact that biblical man thinks in static terms, while we live in an era of evolutionary thought, and consequently we think in dynamic terms. This requires some additional explanation. If you visit the Near East today—Jordan, for example—you find life going on there much as it did in biblical times. The culture is still the same in many ways, as if the clock had stood still. The tools of agriculture are no different from those you see in old pictures which depict the biblical era. Evidently a man who grows up in that kind of a spiritual climate will think more or less statically. He has the feeling that everything has always been that way, and therefore that it must always remain that way. His world is not in fact absolutely stable. In reading the Bible you can see without difficulty that there is a certain growth in culture and in religious thinking. But, after all, the Bible is the distillation of about a thousand years of human history. For someone standing in the midst of it, the hands of the clock are running so slowly that time must seem to be standing still. This makes it difficult for us to understand the Bible, because presently we live in a sort of rapids as far as religion is concerned, and it is only by making a great effort that we can think ourselves into this static way of looking at things. For us it is necessary to translate this static thought, and recast it in terms of growth and evolution. This is no minor problem, because it is often tied up with the most central truths of Christian belief, such questions as original sin, the coming of Christ, and others of similar importance.

The phenomenon of prophecy, as we have said, is subject to these difficulties. The prophets were human beings who had an unusual sensitivity to the breath of the Spirit, and who saw the signs of the times with extraordinary vividness. They had the ability to see behind the facts, and to discover the hand of God in the course of events. History, as far as they were concerned, was salvation history. From this point of view they could make a prognosis of the future, and could unfold God's plan of salvation for their fellow man. One might say that they were blessed with a special instinct for this, somewhat in the way in which a financial wizard can "feel" the way the stock market is going, and can speculate profitably by depending on that instinct. The great pioneer of modern music, the composer Edgar Varese, is supposed to have said that a composer is never ahead of his time—it is the public which is always behind the times. This saying is curious in more ways than one. In the first place, one wonders what else can be meant by "the times," other than the experience of the people who are living at a given time. The most one can say is that some people feel the direction in which men's feeling and thinking are going to develop more quickly than others do. In this sense it is possible to be ahead of one's time. Or, even better, one could say that these are the people who create the times. To a great extent they determine the thinking of the following generation. Especially remarkable is the fact that such people are themselves unaware that they are ahead of their time. Much more often they have the idea that the

rest of mankind has remained behind. The prophets
felt this way, too, but with one significant difference.
While Varese felt that his contemporaries **were** behind, the prophets of the Old Testament, on the other
hand, had the feeling that their fellow men were
deserting, and that they therefore were **falling** behind.
Here again we see a manifestation of the difference
between static and dynamic thinking. The impression
resembles what one experiences when two trains
pull out of the station at the same time on parallel
tracks. It can seem as if the other train is going
backwards while we ourselves are standing still, while
actually just the opposite is true. In the notorious
trial of Galileo something like this took place. The
people who accused Galileo 350 years ago because
he declared that the earth rotated round the sun
believed that they themselves were standing still,
while in fact they were caught up in a complex of
motions. But, those who now condemn the church
leaders of that day forget that they would probably
themselves have been on the same side, because
prophets are ahead of their time. Most of them are
not recognized until after their death, by which time
public opinion has caught up with them. This is the
light in which we must look at the critical words of
Jesus, part of which we have used at the head of this
chapter: "Alas for you, scribes and Pharisees, you
hypocrites! You will build the sepulchres of the
prophets and decorate the tombs of holy men, saying,
'We would never have joined in shedding the blood
of the prophets, had we lived in our fathers' day'"
(Matt. 23:29-30, AV).

Naturally, Israel, too, had its times of falling away. Evolution never rules out degeneration. On the contrary, when we observe the process of evolution, we see that failure is more the rule than the exception. Most of the roads on which evolution sets out are dead ends.[1] It is even likely that the prophets came to their new insights by protesting against the deterioration and the abuse which they saw about them. Yet this deterioration most often had the character of an outgrowth or a festering of something that had originally been a legitimate development. Just as a plant which grows in the wrong kind of atmosphere will go to seed and fester, so religious practices can easily deteriorate when they no longer have the right climate. If you study the history of religious practice, and especially the history of monastic rules, you will find that religious practices easily petrify when they are copied but no longer retain the source of their original nourishment, or are transplanted from the place in which they were first nurtured. It is the same with the misinterpretations and abuses of religion which the prophets condemn. They are often the remains of what had once been healthy developments, but which have become overgrown and turned into monstrosities by excessive cultivation.

Perhaps we should illustrate this fact with a number of examples from the history of God's people, before we turn to the development of the idea of law in Israel. Thus we are accustomed to thinking of the prophets as the defenders of monotheism, the adoration of the one true God. They condemn Israel for unfaithfulness because she has left her lawful bridegroom and gone whoring with the idols of other peoples.

> Yes, their mother has played the whore,
> she who conceived them has disgraced herself.
> "I am going to court my lovers," she said
> "Who give me my bread and water,
> my wool, my flax, my oil, and my drink."
>
> Hosea 2:7

> If a man divorces his wife and she leaves him to marry someone else, may she still go back to him? Has not that piece of land been totally polluted? And you, who have prostituted yourself with so many lovers, you would come back to me?—it is Yahweh who speaks.
>
> Jeremiah 3:1

However, it is a fact that as long as Israel was leading a nomadic existence she was scarcely aware of the existence of other peoples. In any case, she did not know the language of the tribes, and therefore did not know of the existence of other gods. It is as if Israel had been monotheistic by the nature of the case, but when Israel became a settled, agricultural people instead, and as she learned the languages of Canaan, she got to know the gods of Canaan. Israel's monotheism appeared to be incapable of resisting contact with other religions. And at the same time, this shows that Israel's monotheism had always been latently polytheistic. The situation is comparable to that of a young man who has been brought up in a protected Catholic environment and who, on first contact with the non-Christian world, makes an about face and discards his faith. He seems to have lost something, but in fact little or nothing has been lost. What has really happened is that it has been made evident that there was little or nothing there in the first place. Something of the same kind might also be said about the current decline in priestly vocations.

The prophets are renowned also as foes of idolatry. Their mockery of idols provides us with some of the juiciest passages of the Old Testament, and we cannot resist the temptation of citing one of them:

> For the common man it [the tree] is so much fuel; he uses it to warm himself, he also burns it to bake his bread. But this fellow makes a god of it and worships it; he makes an idol of it and bows down before it. Half of it he burns in the fire, on the live embers he roasts meat, eats it and is replete. He warms himself too. "Ah!" says he "I am warm! I have a fire here!" "With the rest he makes his god, his idol; he bows down before it and worships and prays to it.
>
> Isaiah 44:15-17; cf. Wisdom 13:10-19

It will also be obviously clear that the life of a nomadic tribe scarcely offers opportunity for the development of the plastic arts and that in this phase of culture there will hardly have been any place for image worship.

The prophets also put themselves as the champions of the oppressed classes, and the pleaders for social justice. Amos is the best example of this. His prophecy is one long condemnation of the rich, who stretch

themselves out on their ivory couches in their houses
of hewn stone:

> because they trample on the heads of ordinary
>   people
> and push the poor out of their path,
> because father and son have both resorted to
>   the same girl,
> profaning my holy name,
> because they stretch themselves out by the
>   side of every altar
> on clothes acquired as pledges,
> and drink the wine of the people they have
>   fined
> in the house of their god . . . .
>   Amos 2:7-8; cf. 5:11; 6:4

As long as Israel was leading a purely nomadic
life, and the tribal relationship was strong, these
frightful abuses could not occur. It is only in a
settled existence, and with the development of agriculture, that the accumulation of property can occur,
leading to a fixed difference in status between rich
and poor. But the rich, who thus become the oppressors of the poor, have been oppressors potentially in
their hearts all along. When industrialization pro-
vided new ways of acquiring capital, toward the end
of the last century, a great many Christians seemed
to have no idea that property brought with it responsibility. And the workers who were then oppressed
do not now in turn understand that their improved
social position has its consequences with respect to
those who are still worse off.

In the nomadic culture, individual family life as
we know it does not exist. The men of the tribe herd

the cattle together and go together on the hunt. The women of the tribe have more contact with one another than with their own husbands. It is only with the settled existence that family life as we know it begins to develop. We see this clearly in the idealistic description of it in Genesis 2:24: "This is why a man leaves his father and mother and joins himself to his wife, and they become one body." The prophet who wrote that is so far ahead of his time that his story finds scarcely any echo in all the rest of Old Testament writing. It remains in suspended animation until New Testament times, when St. Paul takes up the forgotten melody again (Eph. 5:31).

We could bring forward countless additional examples to show that the prophets who accused their contemporaries of defection were not aware that they were in fact the heralds of a new understanding of God and a new concept of religion. Just one more example, one that is fundamental in the development of Israel's belief and, in truth, in that of every religion, and one which leads us directly to the development of a concept of the law. We are speaking of the transition from the more external, ritualistic religion to a "worship in spirit and truth" (John 4:23).

It is a commonplace of nearly all the prophets that they reject sacrifice. We cannot present all the texts here, but will mention the most elaborate repository, which is Psalm 50, in which, in the guise of a court proceeding, the contemporary cult of sacrifice is found guilty. The expression of the prophet Isaiah is no less intense:

> Hear the word of Yahweh,
> you rulers of Sodom;
> listen to the command of our God,
> you people of Gomorrah.
> What are your endless sacrifices to me?
> says Yahweh.
> I am sick of holocausts of rams
> and the fat of calves.
> The blood of bulls and goats revolts me.
> When you come to present yourselves
>   before me,
> Who asked you to trample over my courts?
> Bring me your worthless offerings no more,
> the smoke of them fills me with disgust.
> New Moons, sabbaths, assemblies—
> I cannot endure festival and solemnity,
> Your New Moons and your pilgrimages
> I hate with all my soul.
> They lie heavy on me,
> I am tired of bearing them.
>   Isaiah 1:10-14

In days gone by, free-thinking exegetes gladly pointed to the prophets as champions of a religionless Christianity, of a religion without worship. The contrast between priest and prophet was depicted as irreconcilable (often enough the opposition between Catholicism and Protestantism stood implicitly in the background.) The Catholic exegete relied, not without reason, on the phrase in some earlier translations, "festival together with misdeeds." The prophets had not set themselves against the worship of the temple in itself, but against the increasing externalization of the sacrificial rites, as a result of which the quantity of offering was perversely equated with the degree of inner religious devotion. It would be an injustice to the great prophets to ignore the fact that they confined their condemnations to the abuses which had come to be associated with what is otherwise a legitimate form of religious expression. At the same time, they represent a new religious feeling to which their contemporaries had not yet attained. And the abuses they condemn are no mere superficial manifestation, separable from the sacrificial practices themselves; they are true manifestations of degeneracy, the precipitate of a phase of religious thought that had had its day.

Primitive man experiences himself as a complete unity of soul and spirit. For this reason the physical is experienced very strongly as an expression of the whole person; so much so that a distinction between the inner meaning and the external deed is not yet possible. In the Bible there are traces of this as yet underdeveloped stage of moral consciousness. Though we do not plan to go into this attitude extensively here, we might suggest that it would be worthwhile to try to find out how much of this can still be found in Catholic religious life. The following two examples will provide a helpful background to our study of the reaction of the prophets to this sort of thinking.[2]

The Bible sets forth a whole series of sacrifices for the washing away of unintentional trespasses (Lev. 4:22, 27; 5:2, 4, 15, 17; Num. 15:27). The so-called cloister rules of Qumran also set forth excommunication as a punishment for unintentional errors.[3] The passage in Numbers to which we have referred makes

it quite clear that Israel knows how to make a
distinction between "sins committed with the hand
raised" for which the penalty is excommunication,
and involuntary "trespasses." The very word "tres-
pass" is definitive, for one can step across a boundary
without being aware of it. Yet, in older books, such
as Samuel, involuntary trespasses are repeatedly
punished by death. The best-known occurrence is
the story of Uzzah (2 Sam. 6:6), who touched the ark
of the Covenant in a purely automatic reaction when
it was in danger of toppling off the wagon in which
it was being carried. We have no way of knowing
exactly what happened, but the relevant thing is that
the writer represents the execution Uzzah to be just
punishment for his involuntary deed. Israel's fear con-
cerning involuntary sins is revealed in the oft-repeated
prayer: "But who can detect his own failings? / Wash
out my hidden faults" (Ps. 19:12). Compare this with
the practice of confessing all our unremembered sins
in the Confessional. We may well wonder if this is
far removed from the Old Testament concept of sin.

The other side of this coin would be the assertion
that there is no such thing as a sin of the mind. There
are reputed exegetes who assert that any ethic of
the will is totally lacking in the Old Testament. The
Tenth Commandment, "You shall not covet . . ." ought
to be translated, "You must not hanker after . . ." with
the implication of making some effort to get the other
fellow's property into your own hands. Whatever the
case may be, it was not without reason that Jesus
stressed the reprehensible nature of sinful desires in

the Sermon on the Mount (Matt. 5:22-27). We have not made much progress here, either. The average Christian has never heard of the sins of desire. Oh, yes, sexual desire is an exception to this, but what we call sexual desire is in fact nearly always erotic fantasy, which is more accurately described as an act than as a desire.

In the final analysis, this is all tied up with a rather formalistic concept of penance. When he has performed the prescribed sacrifices, a person feels very strongly that he has regularized his relationship with God. When David learns that the child of his sin is dead, he gets up off the ground, washes and anoints himself, changes his clothes, and goes into the house of God to pray. Then he has a meal prepared for him, which he eats (2 Sam. 12:20). He has had his punishment, and the incident is closed. This is the kind of mentality you can see to this very day in many "good" Catholics. They make their confessions, and they feel perfectly safe again. It never enters their head that it is supposed to bring them into a completely different relationship with God, namely, of regained love.

If in the time of the prophets Israel still pays little attention to the question of interior ethical disposition, this is not solely or even primarily due to the primitive experience of human existence as a unity of soul and spirit. It is to a large extent the result of the fact that the strength of tribal unity leads to a collective sense of guilt. A strong sense of tribal unity is a fundamental characteristic of nomadic peoples. Naturally, that has its influence on religious thought. The Covenant with Yahweh was concluded, not with an individual, but with an entire people as an entity. Membership in Chosen People was the basis of oneness with God. Consequently, the feeling of sin was also collective. Whenever a law is introduced by the words "I am Yahweh your God who brought you out of the land of Egypt, out of the house of slavery" (Exod. 20:2)—words which call to mind the duties entailed by the Covenant with Israel— the individual clearly feels that he is being spoken to only in his capacity as a member of the people of God. As a generalization, we can actually say that the feeling of responsibility for sin follows hard upon the development of the notion of God. Awareness of sin is like the photographic negative of the understanding of God. Thus it is understandable that in the case of an unsolved murder, expiatory sacrifices had to be offered by the entire community (Deut. 21:1-9).

Development in the direction of a more personal religion, and therefore toward a more individual and a more interior fulfillment of the law was speeded up in Israel by the enormous political catastrophe which we generally call the Babylonian captivity. As national unity went by the boards, a collective sense of guilt inescapably disappeared with it. With this, the burning problem of the suffering of the righteous was born. This suffering could no longer be explained in terms of the sins of the nation. So the problem of retribution sprang into being, the problem which is the central theme of the Book of Job.

The obverse is also the case; one can no longer look to the righteousness of the nation for a way of escaping from God's avenging righteousness, as we read in the Psalms (26:1-2):

> Yahweh, be my judge!
> I go my way in innocence,
> My trust in Yahweh never wavers.
> Test me, Yahweh, and probe me
> put me to the trial, loins and heart; . . .

"The real Jew," St. Paul will say five centuries later, "is the one who is inwardly a Jew, and the real circumcision is in the heart—something not of the letter but of the spirit" (Rom. 2:28-29). Jeremiah and the closely connected Book of Deuteronomy had already announced the same thing:

> Circumcise yourselves for Yahweh;
> off with the foreskin of your hearts.
> Jeremiah 4:4
> Circumcise your heart then
> and be obstinate no longer.
> Deuteronomy 10:16

This is the way by which people come to the conviction that a person is responsible for his own sins, and that people can no longer blame national catastrophes on the sins of their fathers. The great apostle of this new idea was the prophet Ezekiel, who appeared at the time of the Exile. The following passage is very well known. It is found in the liturgy of Lent:

> The fathers have eaten unripe grapes;
> and the children's teeth are set on edge?

As I live—it is the Lord Yahweh who speaks
—there will no longer be any reason to repeat
this proverb in Israel. See now: all life belongs
to me: the father's life and the son's life, both
alike belong to me. The man who has sinned, he
is the one who shall die.

Ezekiel 18:1-4; cf. 33:1-20

In those days people will no longer say:
  "The fathers have eaten unripe grapes;
  the children's teeth are set on edge."
But each is to die for his own sin. Every man
who eats unripe grapes is to have his own teeth
set on edge.

Jeremiah 31:29-30

From this it is only a short step to the idea of the
interior law. Because of the disappearance, of the
community as a normalizing factor, the Israelite was
left in an ethical vacuum. In that age of moral con-
fusion, the prophets rose up to give God's people a
new law, the inward voice of a conscience which was
needed to replace the moral sanctions of the environment. In the first chapter we quoted the wonderful
passage from Deuteronomy (30:11-14) the central idea
of which is: "No, the word is very near to you, it is
in your mouth and in your heart for your observance."
From Jeremiah, too, comes the celebrated passage in
which the New Covenant is spoken of for the first
time: "See, the days are coming—it is Yahweh who
speaks—when I will make a new covenant with the
House of Israel (and the House of Judah), but not a
covenant like the one I made with their ancestors on
the day I took them by the hand to bring them out
of the land of Egypt. They broke that covenant of

mine, so I had to show them who was master. It is Yahweh who speaks. Deep within them I will plant my Law, writing it on their hearts. Then I will be their God and they shall be my people. There will be no further need for neighbour to try to teach neighbour, or brother to say to brother, 'Learn to know Yahweh!' No, they will all know me, the least no less than the greatest—it is Yahweh who speaks—since I will forgive their iniquity and never call their sin to mind" (Jer. 31:31-34).

Ezekiel, too, has this idea, though he makes it less explicit. He already represents a further stage of development: "I shall give you a new heart, and put a new spirit in you; I shall remove the heart of stone from your bodies and give you a heart of flesh instead. I shall put my spirit in you, and make you keep my laws and sincerely respect my ordinances" (Ezek. 36:26-27).

This is where the idea that God has written His law in man's heart comes from. We encounter this idea later in Paul: "For instance, pagans who never heard of the Law but are led by reason[4] to do what the Law commands, may not actually 'possess' the Law, but they can be said to 'be' the Law. They can point to the substance of the Law engraved on their hearts.—they can call a witness, that is, their own conscience—they have accusation·and defense, that is, their own inner mental dialogue" (Rom. 2:14-15).

This is the source of the idea of a "natural law" which God has written into man's heart. It appears

that the development of this idea was helped along
by the fact that Jeremiah draws a parallel with the
"natural laws" of physical nature:

> Yahweh who provides the sun for light by day,
> the moon and stars for light by night,
> who stirs the sea, making its waves roar,
> he whose name is Yahweh Sabaoth, says this:
> Were this established order ever to pass away
> from my presence—it is Yahweh who speaks—
> only then would the race of Israel also cease
> to be a nation in my presence forever.
>
> Jeremiah 31:35-36

Thus this law of nature is also the ideal of true
humanity, the one that God had in mind when He
created mankind, and which He put into man's
nature as an inner teleology. This law is not imposed
upon him from outside, but is a spontaneous flowering
of his personality.

The concept of natural law has tended to be
looked down upon of late. For one reason, ethnolo-
gists have established that such a law of nature can
be found only very fragmentarily in primitive people
who have never been in contact with Christianity.
Almost the only thing they know which compares
with our Ten Commandments are prohibitions against
murder and against certain kinds of sexual inter-
course.[5] And, what is more important, the very
concept of nature in this connection is no longer in
vogue. The nature of a beast can be specified because
it is determined, and it reacts automatically according
to certain laws. But a man is a free being, and
therefore the concept of nature is much vaguer with

respect to him. As a consequence it is also true that the rules which are connected with this nature defy specification. To be sure, we can point out certain fundamental traits of his being. A man is a being who lives in fellowship with others of his kind. Certain rules of the game follow automatically from this, rules which enable this living together to keep on the right track. But man and fellowship are both in a state of continuous development, so it is always exceedingly difficult to make these laws more concrete. A single example as an illustration. The Church has the power to annul a marriage that has not been consummated. Clearly, this law rests upon a particular view of man which assigns a very important place to the physical factors in marriage. According to newer insights, a marriage is a fellowship of persons in love. So one may ask whether a marriage can really be said to have been consummated when that kind of personal relationship has never come into being.

Be that as it may, one cannot really deduce a concept of natural law from the Scriptures. When Jeremiah says that the people of the New Covenant will know God without learning about Him from other men, he is not speaking of any inborn knowledge, but only of the absence of transference of this knowledge from one person to another. Of course, this is an impossibility, but the entire world of the future as envisaged by the prophets is unrealistic. They paint the age of messianic salvation the same way they do the ancient times of Paradise, by thinking

away the evils that are in the world as they know it.
How else could they do it? Paradise is a picture
drawn to contrast with the actual world. By proceeding from a Paradise constructed from the best elements of the sublunar world, the story is made to
show vividly how sin has spoiled everything and is
thus the explanation of the way things now are.[6] It is
clear that in this manner a world comes into being
which does not logically fit together. The same
illogical process is going on here. In a time of exile
and dispersion the idea that one man should be
dependent on another for his knowledge of God seems
like an "evil." Therefore the prophet predicts that
under the New Covenant the intervention of our
fellow man will no longer be necessary to the knowledge of God.

The very term "New Covenant" reveals the fact
that the prophet looks upon the messianic future as
an idealized revival of the past; "New Covenant"
implies renewal of an old past. In chapters 40-48,
Ezekiel describes the new temple with its perfect
worship, an idealization of the old temple. He sees
the Exile as the conclusion of a cycle. God leads
His people into the Promised Land. By their lack of
faith the people call down upon their heads the curse
of Deuteronomy 28, and must therefore go back to
their former nomadic existence: "My father was a
wandering Aramaean" (Deut. 26:5). But after this,
God will beckon and will once more lead Israel out
of the desert wilderness (Isa. 2:13). In this way Israel
will begin the second cycle.[7] This new cycle will be

an idealized repetition of the first, and therefore the much disputed passage in Jeremiah 31:31 is not to be interpreted in such a way as to make the prophet out to be an untimely advocate of situational ethics. It would not fit his frame of reference at all. A covenant requires statutes to which both parties are bound. Even Jesus, though He called himself the prophet of the Most High, did not put himself forward as a reformer of the law. On the contrary, He said He had come, not to get rid of the law, but to fulfill it (Matt. 5:17). When love cools off, it is because lawlessness is on the increase (Matt. 24:12). He was addressed as "Rabbi," the title given to those who are learned in the Scriptures, and quite rightly so, because He was always defending the law, as we shall see in a later chapter.[8]

The mission of Jesus, who was, after all, one of the prophets, did not fail because the Jews were looking for a messianic kingdom which would be an idealized verion of the past. If that had been the reason, they could not have been blamed, because they could not have anticipated anything else; the prophets had never contemplated anything else. And conversely, if it were only a question here of a way of thinking, it would not be so difficult for our generation to give up an older point of view. After all, we have learned to think dynamically, we have come to understand the relativity of human laws. What, then, is left of the laws of the Old Testament which we have heard proclaimed as the law of God? But even with this insight the future lies hidden, and herein lies the difficulty. We know that old certainties fall by the wayside, but we do not know what is going to take their place. We know it as little as the prophets did. In this respect nothing has altered. If man is to be open to new possibilities, he must sacrifice the old certainties, and that demands a great deal of humility and trust. In the depths of his being, man is an enigma, as Ebeling has said. In the last analysis, man is passive in the most fundamental sense of that word, because he is faced with the question of where he comes from, and where he is going. It is summed up in the words: "Adam, where are you?" (Gen. 3:9).[9]

4

"... THE RULES AND DECREES OF THE LAW"

EPHESIANS 2:14

According to Bishop Robinson, the author of
Honest to God, the distinction between Catholic and
Protestant consists in the fact that the Catholic tries
to draw the net tighter and tighter, while the Protestant wants to make the individual cords of the net
stronger.[1] I prefer to express the difference this way:
The Catholic Church is always trying to make the net
finer by increasing the number of laws so that a
completely clear solution is made available for every
conceivable situation. This is an effort which is
doomed in advance to miscarry, because every time
one adds a new string to the net, one adds a new hole,
too.[2] Or, to say this without using a figure of speech,
every new law brings a new definition with it, and
the new definition brings with it a new way of avoiding the law. There is not a single human law that
is one hundred per cent effective. We have already
observed that human words do not precisely reflect
what we think and feel, and that therefore, **a fortiori,**
no human law can ever make God's intention definite
and certain forever.[3] Everything human is relative,
and therefore limited, and every limitation entails a

negation. Every definition excludes other possibilities, like so many still-births. This is another sense in which it is true to say that the letter kills (2 Cor. 3:6). As soon as God's will is translated and cut down to size by putting it into human words, the Spirit becomes as immobile as the stone on which the law of Moses was engraved.

Yet, like Sisyphus, we cannot help trying time and time again to achieve the impossible. The great proliferation of human laws forms the best proof of this impossibility, but at the same time it is the expression of man's ceaseless effort against his own inadequacy. He realizes that he can never stem the flood of life, and therefore he is always building new sea walls to protect the old ones. Outside the walls he has erected to protect the City of God, he builds another wall, and then yet another outside that. The trouble is that the enemy sits inside the walls, for the enemy is, in short, his own human failing. The monastic orders have their rules which aim to protect the brethren against disobeying the Commandments, but beyond that there is the customs book which is meant to prevent one from breaking the rule which in turn is meant to prevent one from breaking the Commandment.

This business of constantly devising new rules is ultimately an expression of human pride. Man is unable to stomach his disenchantment with his own failings, and so he tries to anchor his life with regulations and formulas, in order to create the illusion that everything is in order and, even more important, so he can point the finger at the obvious disorderliness of the other fellow. Whenever life is precisely delineated by laws and regulations, a man can feel that he is master of the situation. He can put his thumb in his waistcoat pocket and say, "I have done everything that could be expected of me." Even more important than that, he has a standard by which he can judge and condemn the other fellow, and this judgment of his neighbor gives him that wonderful feeling, "I thank you, God, that I am not like the rest of mankind, and particularly that I am not like this tax collector here" (Luke 18:11), a feeling in which the self-reproach of his own sense of insufficiency is swallowed up.

Whenever the prophets long for the impossible by predicting that the law of God will one day be freed from human doctrine, it is because they are acutely aware that Israel's culture is going bad. They foresee intuitively that God's people are going to tie themselves up in knots, and will at long last suffocate in their own laws and traditions. Their longing for a Savior who will free man is in large measure a homesickness for the law which will come forth from Zion, that is to say, out of God's own heart (Isa. 2:3). Furthermore, it is a longing for the time when men will no longer do harm, and will no longer work evil, because the earth will be full of the knowledge of Yahweh as the waters swell the sea (Isa. 11:9).

Bishop Robinson, whom we quoted above, comments that the first canon of Church law, which was proclaimed by the Council of Jerusalem (Acts 15:22-29),

was already out of date before the ink was dry.
"Whenever I think of this during a meeting of Synod,
I get quite perked up," he says.[4] This was the Church's
first attempt at **aggiornamento,** and it is a most
instructive illustration of what we have just said. At
the same time, the Council clearly illuminated the
Jewish attitude toward the law of that era, that is, of
the last centuries before Christ. The Book of the Acts
is nothing less than the story of the Church's awakening to self-consciousness, and therefore of her coming
into being. And this achievement of consciousness
occurred in much the same way it does in a human
child as it grows up: by confrontation with a "thou."
In this case, the "thou" is the Jewish past. The story
of this awakening is at the same time a story of
freedom, because as people become free, they become
aware of their selfhood. So the Church had to guarantee the victory of Christian freedom over the past.
This is reason enough for paying a certain amount of
attention to this Council.

The decrees of this Council are usually called the
Apostolic Decrees. Luke mentions these decrees in
three different places (Acts 15:20, 29; 21:25), which
shows how important he thinks they are. This throws
some light on the Council itself as well. Luke seems
to have tied together a number of separate discussions
of the question and described them as if they had
taken place at a single solemn session, so as to make
the question stand out more clearly. He considered it
an extremely important event in the Church's development. To others, especially Paul, the decrees evi-

dently did not have a comparable significance, because they are not referred to, even when Paul is
speaking about this very subject.

It is strange that these definitions which Luke
thinks are so important have come down to us in
such careless manuscripts. It is not just that the order
of the decrees is different each time, but that several
of the manuscripts have a substantially different version. The issue in question is, Must a gentle cate-
chumen keep the Jewish law? Or, to put it another
way, Must one become a Jew before he can become
a Christian? The answer seems obvious enough to us,
but to the apostles, all born Jews, it was not at all
evident. After all, it was a question of the law of
God. Was not Judaism the foundation of the Church,
and were not the Gentiles sanctified by being grafted
on to the stem of God's people? (Rom. 11:16-24).
But, on the other hand, it would have been impossible
to teach these newly converted pagans the entire
Jewish law. And even if one could have taught it to
them, it would have been impossible to arrange to
have them keep it in the midst of a pagan community.
Worse than that, even the Jews themselves had come
to the conclusion that they could not keep this law
consistently. Peter said, "It would only provoke God's
anger . . . if you imposed on the disciples the very
burden that neither we nor our ancestors were strong
enough to support" (Acts 15:10). (One should realize
that the apostle was of a Galilean family which had
intimately experienced the difficulty of keeping the
law in a semipagan environment.) In consequence

they decided to choose a middle way, and to require of the neophytes only those laws to which, in theory at least, non-Jews living in Palestine were held. These were the so-called laws of Noah, which tradition ascribed to the time of Noah, and which were said to have been imposed on him after the flood, and which therefore applied to all his descendants. These laws required abstinence from meat that had been offered to idols; forbade marriage within certain degrees of kinship, which extended further among the Jews than among the heathen; and prohibited the eating of blood or of meat from which the blood had not been drained.

The manuscripts we mentioned above omit the rule against strangled meat, and in place of it they put the so-called Golden Rule, "Do to no one what you would not want done to you" (cf. Tob. 4:16 and Matt. 7:12). They make the substitution in each of the three places where the decisions appear, perhaps with a view to retaining the count of four. What is the intention here? It surely seems as if the definitions of the Council were outdated very fast. Perhaps they never were applied throughout the entire Church, which is what we might also deduce from the writings of Paul. But, on the other hand, people were not willing simply to omit these passages, so they twisted the ritual laws into moral prescriptions. The eating of meat offered to idols was understood as idolatry. Blood was understood to mean murder; and for marriage within the forbidden degrees they understood, in a word, all unlawful cohabitation, which is to say, adultery. But no one could figure out what to do with the one about strangled meat, so they just had to leave it out and put the Golden Rule in its place. This example is relevant in more than one way. It seems in the first place that the sovereign freedom with which the young Church had simply set aside the law of Moses must quickly have given way to an attitude of holding on for dear life, resulting in some rather farfetched efforts to save the letter of the law when there was no longer the slightest chance of its being saved. But even more astonishing is the freedom itself, dealing as it did with nothing more or less than the very law of God. The desperate efforts of the later Fathers to explain the law as symbolic, and thus to save the letter of the law, only serve to underscore this fact, and to indicate that people genuinely recognized the gravity of this decision. It could not be evaded by pointing to the fact that Jesus had done way with the law. In the next chapter we shall see that this is exactly what He did not do.

At the same time, the decrees of the Apostolic Council reveal a deeply human side of the Church. The fact that they were a compromise explains why they were out of date even before they were promulgated. But it was evidently not humanly possible to abandon the whole law at one stroke, even though that was the only possible logical result of what was already beginning to happen. In order to win the cooperation of the opposition party, therefore, several exceptions were made, which in fact still meant a total abandonment of the law. For the same forces which were at work in this process now aim together at these last remnants. We cannot help thinking here about the recent changes in the rules for the Eucharistic fast, and other similar changes. We could wish that the Church could have abolished them in a clean-cut way, instead of leaving the bare skeleton lying about in the form of rules to which nobody pays any attention anyway. But evidently that was not yet possible, and they had to work out a compromise in the conviction that the course of events would take care of the rest.

All the same, it is a quite remarkable fact that the law of Moses could have been dealt with in such an unabashed way, with all the age-long tradition which surrounded it like a nimbus, with all its reputation for divine unapproachability. Yet the Church was in fact able to do away with the greater portion of it. The vital importance of this step is no longer within our immediate sphere of experience, so we cannot visualize the psychological significance of the step. Therefore, we have to seek an explanation; for to attribute this development simply to the working of the Holy Spirit would be dangerous supernaturalism. It would rob this unparalleled example of any worth that it may have for the Church of today.

In part, the courageous attitude of the Church can be explained by the example which Jesus himself gave, because, even though He never rejected so much as one single law, He exhibited a superhuman liberalism when it came to interpreting and applying the law, as, for example, in the case of the Sabbath being made for man, and not man for the Sabbath (Mark 2:27). Yet this saying of Jesus could never have been understood, nor could it have been handed down as a tradition, unless the time had been ripe for it. So this is another respect in which we can say that He came in the fullness of time.

Humanly speaking, we can explain this unique event, one which was never to be repeated in the history of the Church, only in the light of the fact that the weight of the Commandments had at long last become so totally unbearable that the whole house of cards which constituted the law and tradition was ready to fall down of its own weight. The plaster work of continually refined oral interpretation had by that time become so thick that it fell down in great chunks, leaving the bare walls exposed.

Alas, people will not tolerate those bare walls. But instead of pulling them down, they normally set about replastering them with a vengeance. Hence the story repeats itself over and over again, with intermissions. It should be extremely helpful to analyze the factors which led to such a development because, if the signs of the times are not deceiving us, we are in the midst of a similar phase today. Many law-abiding Christians are greatly frightened when they see how loose the plaster work is on every side, and how when one piece falls it takes another one with it.

Several factors which went into this oblique development of the Jewish concept of law could be pointed out. It is difficult to give an orderly description of the process, because cause and effect are continually overlapping. Perhaps the following is the best that can be done: The people of the Covenant become also the people of the law. Originally the keeping of the law is man's answer to God's grace in the Covenant, and not the other way round, because whenever God concludes a Covenant with the people of Israel it means that He is binding himself to that people in a special way; the law merely serves to protect that tie against breakage, since breaking with God means death to man. God does not choose His people because they are better than other peoples: "If Yahweh set his heart on you and chose you, it was not because you out-numbered other peoples: you were the least of all peoples. It was for love of you and to keep the oath he swore to your fathers that Yahweh brought you out with his mighty hand and redeemed you from the house of slavery, from the power of Pharaoh king of Egypt" (Deut. 7:7-8). Therefore the announcement of the law always begins with the summation of God's gracious deeds: "I am Yahweh your God who brought you out of the land of Egypt, out of the house of slavery. You shall have no gods except me" (Deut. 5:6; cf. 6:4; 10:12-13, and so on). Even in later writings, the law still is called "the book of the Covenant" (1 Macc. 1:57; Sirach 24:23).

Naturally the idea of the Covenant, which was sealed according to the example of a political agreement, remains always somewhat juridical in character. Further, it cannot be denied, in my opinion, that the Jewish spirit has a natural attraction to legal

quibblings. Harry Mulisch (himself half-Jewish) writes
in this context: "Jews have long had a 'juridic-
telekinetic' attitude toward reality. Characteristic
enough their relationship with their God is also of
juridical nature, governed by laws and commandments: Moses, the Talmud. They are never entirely
absorbed in their God; they stand not in contact with
God, but in contract with God. . . . This exceptionally
non-mystical Jewish spirit has still produced three
genuises, who have successfully changed the society,
nature and man with their laws: Marx, Einstein and
Freud. The common characteristic of all these Jewish
'lawgivers' is that with their **understanding** they pene-
trate to a point where that had been considered to
be impossible: to areas which **before** these men's
appearance had belonged to the 'mystical.' "⁵ And
yet in all honesty, in my opinion, we must dig to a
deeper level. It is a fundamental human need for
man to "regulate" his relationship with the invisible
forces in order in this way to get a hold on them.
The idea of a covenant does not in itself rule out
independence. In the ancient East when a great king
sealed a covenant with a vassal, that was primarily
a manifestation of good will, thus of grace.

The same thing may be said about wages or
earnings. In contrast to Paul, Jesus himself did not
hesitate to use this figure of speech. It is an evidence
of God's trust that He has put this dangerous toy
into man's hand. It must be said that the idea of
wages is not really compatible with the concept of
law. The lawgiver sets down penalties for transgress-

ing, for failing to keep the law. But the idea of
promising a reward for keeping the law never enters
any judge's head. The fact that such a thing did
happen in the later Jewish concept of the law indicates that something has gone wrong. For one reason
or another, the law has become separated from the
great unity of the Covenant with Yahweh, and has
attained to an independent magnitude. In this process,
the personal connection with God has been lost. God
is no longer thought of as choosing man by his grace,
but man is thought of as having chosen the side of
the law because the law has pleased him well (Ps.
1:2), and because the law is a delight and a refresh-
ment to him (Ps. 119:70, 77, 92, 174). What had
originally been an evidence of dependence, and thus
essentially of being someone else's property, had now
become something men possess for themselves: "We
have a law."

In the psalms we have just cited, each section of
which is a song in praise of the law, the word "covenant" does not appear at all. This is most evident in
Psalm 119, the longest of all the psalms, which consists of 22 stanzas of 8 verses each, in each of which
the word "law" or a synonym is found. It is a litany
in praise of the law. It is only in Psalm 50 (vs. 16)
and in Psalm 78 (vs. 10) that we still find a connection
between law and Covenant. The situation is the
same in Ezekiel. In the third section of the book,
chapters 40-48, which gives a detailed description of
the new temple and the new worship, the word
"covenant" is to be found only once, and then in a

negative sense, for it is the Covenant which the house of Israel has violated (44:7).

Along with this, the idea of covenant has become degraded, because in later times all sorts of things are called covenants, and are given a place beside **The** Covenant: the covenant with Noah (Gen. 9:8-17), with Abraham (Gen. 17:2), with David (2 Sam. 7:8-9; 23:1-7; Ps. 89:4, 29, 35, 40), with Levi (Mal. 2:4-5, 8; Neh. 13:29; Dan. 11:22).

The shift is clearly reflected in worship. In the old tabernacle, the ark of the Covenant was the central thing. God dwelt above the ark, hidden in the mysterious cloud, the shekinah, which floated above the cherubs on the lid of the ark (Exod. 25:17-21). This ark, or better still its lid, was the footstool of the invisible God who sat upon the cherubs like an eastern Prince (1 Sam. 4:4; Ps. 80:2; 99:1). The tables of the law, which lay in the ark (Deut. 10:4-5) had only a secondary place. In olden times they put a sort of safe in which contracts could be filed away under the statues of the gods, so as to place them under a kind of divine guarantee. This is why the tablets of the law were put into the ark, but the most important part of the ark was the lid, which was called "lid of atonement" because it had a central place in the ceremonial of the great Day of Atonement (Lev. 16:2, 12-16). The Holy of Holies itself was even called the House of the Lid of Reconciliation (1 Chron. 28:11).

After the Exile, when the temple had been

destroyed, the synagogue took its place, and was called Beth ha Midrash, or "House of Study"—in Yiddish, **schul,** meaning simply "school." The priests and Levites appointed by God to offer sacrifice now became the teachers of the law (2 Chron. 17:7-9; 19:8-10; 35:3; Neh. 8:5-8). Jeremiah's expression in 18:18 is noteworthy in this connection: ". . . the priest will not run short of instruction . . . nor the sage of advice, nor the prophet of the word." It would seem from this that instruction in the law had by that time become the specific task of the priest. "Many a day Israel will spend without a faithful God, without priest to teach, without law" (2 Chron. 15:3). The bookcase which contains the holy books now becomes the central point of worship, taking the place of the altar of sacrifice, while the priest becomes the servant of the Word. In this way the law takes on an absolute importance, and even takes the place of God himself. The alliance with the living God is obscured, which results in a great loss for faith. So the origin of the law becomes obscured, and the law itself becomes a nameless, tyrannical power without a face, to such an extent that Paul can identify it with the elements of this world (Gal. 4:9; Col. 2:8), the powers of the rulers of this world of darkness (Eph. 6:12) from which Christ has freed us.

Accompanying this development and accelerating it are a number of secondary phenomena which have caused the calcification to take on freakish forms. In the second chapter of this book we showed how Israel expressed the transcendence of law by ascribing the entire book of law, civil law included, to God himself. This had the fatal result of losing sight of the fact that laws form a mutually interdependent hierarchy. Every law becomes without distinction the law of God—one exactly as important as the next. When the scribe in the Gospel asks Christ which is the greatest law, he is not asking a question about the order of pre-eminence of the laws. The question he raises is purely academic. He is asking which is the law from which all the others can be derived. But when the events of daily life give rise to a conflict between two or more laws, the only relevant question from the point of view of the scribe is, which law is the most surely applicable. This is a matter to which we will return in the next chapter, for it is one of the points against which Jesus of Nazareth protested most outspokenly. We also pointed out that many of the ordinances of the law of Moses derived from what are called casuistic laws. The ones that are introduced by the phrase "Suppose that someone" came into existence from the practice of jurisprudence. A result of this is that they are infimately tied up with the problems of the age from which they sprang, and they easily become outdated. Having been canonized as laws of God, they claimed eternal worth; but, on the other hand, they were no longer of any practical value. What should be done with them? The answer was to interpret them in an artificial way, so that the letter of the law could be preserved. Sometimes this artificiality was extended to laws that were not really obsolete, giving rise to a hollow formalism. One of the most unhappy examples of this formalism and literalism is given in the Gospel (Mark 7:11ff.): "If a man says to his father or mother: Anything I have that I might have used to help you is Corban (that is, dedicated to God) then he is forbidden from that moment to do anything for his father or mother." This is no isolated example. For instance, on the Sabbath day one was not allowed to walk more than a certain distance, a "Sabbath day's journey." But the scribes invented a fictitious residence, called Erub, so that you could walk a Sabbath day's journey past the Erub without desecration.

It is self-evident that the understanding of finding ways of evasion like that was a science in itself, and the exclusive possession of the scribes. To safeguard their monopoly they went further and further in the devising of subtle distinctions. One has only to read the tractate on the Sabbath to create an anthology of futility. Was one allowed to eat an egg that had been laid on the Sabbath, the hen having violated the Sabbath by working to produce the egg? One was not allowed to kill an animal, but was one allowed to kill a flea? The stricter interpretation was that it would be a detestable violation of the Sabbath to do so. The more liberal opinion was that one could cut the legs off the little beast, so that one could kill it more conveniently when the Sabbath was over. To enlarge this anthology any further would be uncharitable. But, as a matter of fact, one could just as easily put together this kind of anthology from our own ecclesiastical law. For example, would one break the Eucharistic fast if he deliberately inhaled the

aroma of something edible? Or if one got water down
his throat while brushing his teeth? Questions like
this can easily be found in our old manuals. There,
too, legalism has become a kind of sport, and at the
same time a kind of secret knowledge of specialists.
In view of this, the desire of the prophets for a
knowledge of God which does not depend on man
is entirely understandable, for the study of this law
had been given into the hands of certain privileged
people, and the rest of mankind was doomed to live
in sin (John 7:29). What is more, the Exile had con-
tributed to the externalization of the law. This may
at first sight seem odd, but it is a well-known conclusion of sociology that a minority people require
external practices in order to protect their identity
against the world outside. These heighten the group's
self-awareness and make its continuity possible. And
this is true for a religious group as well as for any
other. The result is that laws which serve as distinc-
tive signs of the group receive an undeservedly strong
emphasis. As everyone knows, in predominantly
Catholic countries, the Sunday obligation is taken
much less seriously than it is in pluralistic countries
like Holland or the United States. We can detect a
similar phenomenon in postexilic Judaism, especially
where the law of the Sabbath is concerned, as well
as with regard to circumcision and the dietary laws,
which take on an extraordinary importance under
such conditions. In order to give these laws greater
weight, their origin is projected back into the gray
past. The first creation narrative with its six days
of work is meant to date the observance of the

Sabbath to the beginning of the world, and thus to make it into the most important of the Commandments. The command to abstain from blood is put back to the days of the flood, while circumcision is attributed to Abraham. At the time of the Maccabean fight for freedom, thousands of Jews let themselves be slaughtered because they refused to defend themselves on the Sabbath. Eleazar and the seven Maccabee brothers died because they refused to eat pork. Against this background, it is understandable that Jesus finds himself in conflict especially with the laws of the Sabbath and of ritual purity, while Paul turns with especial vehemence against circumcision and the dietary laws. For the reasons just described, these laws have grown out of all proportion to their normal importance, so that the mutual order of the various laws was most severly disturbed at this point.

For this reason, too, the laws become a purely nationalistic matter, so that even the non-Jewish regime has to begin to be concerned about them. The Persian king named Esdras to the post of secretary of the law of the God of heaven (Esdras 7:12-21), and Darius II (419 B.C.) of Persia regulated the celebration of Passover for the community of the dispersion near Elephantine.[6] In this way the law turns into a wall of separation which hermetically seals off the world of the Jew from the world of the heathen (Eph. 2:17). This is one of the reasons why Paul became a partisan of the fight against the law. As apostle to the Gentiles, he experienced the extent to which this Jewish law interfered with the missionary effort. God had made the Covenant with Israel in order to achieve a relationship with all men by means of the Jewish people. Israel was, so to speak, the bridgehead of salvation from which God aimed to create for himself a liberated people, but Israel had foresworn its destiny by keeping the gift of the Covenant jealously for itself, thus making the law into a gate with which it shut off the rest of humanity from salvation.

The law brought not only separation between Israel and the rest of the world; it slowly but surely brought a spiritual division within Israel itself. On the one hand, there were the official leaders of the people who did not hesitate to make a pact with the Roman overlords in order to safeguard their own position. Ultimately they committed the greatest of all judicial murders in the name of the law: "We have a law . . . and according to that law he ought to die" (John 19:7). But on the other side were a large group of quiet country people who, having been purified by the Exile and later persecutions, applied themselves to fulfilling the law so that the coming of Messiah might be hastened. They did not regard the law as a crushing burden, any more than the Orthodox Jew of today does, having grown up in the law from childhood, and having learned to accept it as an ingrained habit. The classical Yiddish author Jitschok Leib Peretz (1851-1915), in his tale **Peace** describes the "joy in the law" which such men experience; but at the same time he also reveals the conflict of conscience of the man who cannot follow all the scholarly arguments.[7]

Chaim, the porter, has listened to the learned commentaries of the rabbi, and he sighs, "Lord of the world, if I could only have a little scrap of Paradise for myself, my wife, and my children!" and he becomes sad, and wonders, "But on account of what merit, why, what for, an unworthy fellow like me?" Once, after study, he goes to the rabbi: "Rabbi," he says with a trembling voice, "give me some advice as to how I can receive the privilege of entering paradise."

"Study the holy doctrine, my son," was the answer.
"I can't."
"Study the commentary on the Talmud, the Ayin Jacob, or even the Pirke Aboth."
"I can't."
"Then recite the Psalms."
"I haven't any time for that."
"Pray earnestly."
"I don't understand what I'm praying."
The rabbi looked at him with deep sympathy. "What do you do for a living?"
"I'm a porter."
"All right, serve the scholars."
"What do you mean by that?"
"Well, for example, bring a couple of jars of water to the house of study every evening so the scholars will have something to drink."
Chaim brightened up. "What about my wife, Rabbi?" he asked.
"If a man sits on a chair in Paradise, his wife is his footstool."

When Chaim came home for the ringing out of the Sabbath he found his wife sitting in a chair reciting the prayer, God of Abraham. A pang went through his heart when he saw her. "No, Chana," he burst out, "I won't have you be my footstool. I'll bend down and raise you up and seat you beside me. We shall sit together in one chair, and the Lord of the World will have to be content with it."

No doubt Zachariah and his wife Elisabeth were people like this, of whom Luke writes so sympathetically that they were both just people and lived blamelessly according to all the laws and commands of the Lord. They had only one desire, and that was to be free from the power of the enemy so they could serve the Lord without fear, in holiness and righteousness before His countenance all the days of their life (Luke 1:64-65). And it was of such folk that the Rabbi of Nazareth was born, who was to free His people from the curse of the law. But He had first of all to become a curse himself (Gal. 3:13).

5

"I HAVE COME NOT
TO ABOLISH . . ."

MATTHEW 5:17

There have always been people who were convinced that the profusion of human laws was a
necessary evil. Necessary because of man's imper-
fection, and yet an evil because it is something that
really should not be so. The most poetic expression
of man's nostalgia for Godly simplicity of life is found
in the story of Paradise. In our third chapter we
showed, quite incidentally, that the author of this
story created a paradisial world by imagining the
world with which he himself was familiar with the
evil deleted from it. It is quite evident that among
the shortcomings of this world, he numbered the
great profusion of laws and commandments. He felt
this to be something evil which the Creator could
never have intended to be the way it is. On the
other hand, it was clear to him that even in Paradise
man was a creature, and therefore could not have
existed entirely without laws. But this creaturely dependence was not an oppressive burden for man in
Paradise. So it came about that the writer of this
narrative envisaged a moral order with only a single
interdiction. And, moreover, this proscription was

such a pointless one that later writers have always been tempted to look for some hidden meaning behind it, and most commonly they made it out to be a euphemism for an edict against sexual relations. But if one accepts this, he misses the point. This picture of Paradise was painted precisely in order to show that God's commandments should really be a light burden on us.

Jesus Christ is the fulfillment of the messianic prophecies, the end of the law and its fulfillment at one and the same time. When we keep this in mind, we will not be surprised to encounter again and again the assertion that Jesus has abolished the law of Moses, as the well-known professor Monsignor L. Cerfaux of Louvain writes: "The agreement between the attitude of Christ and that of the Apostle [Paul] is striking. Christ declares that the Law has in part fallen away, for example, as far as resting on the Sabbath is concerned. Paul will later do the same."[1] Some scholars go even further, claiming that Jesus has never been completely understood by the Church. The later community having been frightened off by the radicalism of Jesus has normalized His all too daring pronouncements. They speak of the Church as re-Judaizing.[2] Catholic scholars have usually chosen a middle course. Jesus did away with the civil and ritual laws, but maintained the moral law:[3] a distinction of which no trace is to be found in the Bible.

Meanwhile there is not a single place in all of the New Testament where we can say with certainty that Jesus has swept a law aside, not even where the

Sabbath is concerned. It appears to be essential for us to look into the most important evidences for this, not merely for historical reasons but because this is a question of practical importance for our own time. The Christian of today needs to learn how he can keep his inner freedom despite the existence of antiquated and encrusted laws. Most important of all, we need to understand how an honest striving for reform can go hand in hand with childlike obedience to the law as an expression of the will of God.

Time and time again Jesus found himself in conflict with His contemporaries' understanding of the law of the Sabbath. This was, in fact, the chief area of conflict between Him and the scribes. We can demonstrate this statistically, for the word "sabbath" appears fifty-six times in the New Testament, and nearly every time it is in a situation of conflict. Surely the best place to start is with the story of the disciples plucking the ears of grain, and it is here that we find the fundamental declaration: "The sabbath was made for man, not man for the sabbath" (Mark 2:27). Matthew adds to the story that the disciples were hungry (Matt. 12:1). It seems that he wants to soften the antagonistic character of the story for the sake of his Jewish readers. It is a fair comment, all the same, as Jesus' own defense shows: David himself ate of the shewbread in case of need, even though in principle it was reserved for the priests. Actually, the "need" was not so great in this case. David was living in the wilderness, but the disciples could easily have waited until sundown. The case of David could be

called an example of situational ethics. Every law
presumes the normal situation, but necessity stands
above the law. There are situations which the lawgiver could not have foreseen, unless he had wanted
to make as many laws as there are possible situations.
What Jesus did was not simply to apply this principle.
The Jews were already quite familiar with it, and
appealed in cases like it to a rule that was almost
word for word the same: "The sabbath was intended
for you, and not you for the sabbath."[4] But that was
a rule which applied only when life was actually in
danger. Jesus means more by it. He re-establishes
the original intent of the law by appealing to an
accepted principle. The Sabbath was established so
that there would be a regularly recurring day of rest
for man and beast. The Sabbath was intended for
man's well-being. Thus Matthew was right to add at
the end: "If you had understood the meaning of the
words: 'What I want is mercy, not sacrifice,' you
would not have condemned the blameless" (Matt.
12:7). But the legalism of the scribes had turned
this day of rejoicing into a scarcely tolerable burden,
rather like what Sunday used to be in days gone by,
a day of endless boredom for the Christian.[5] And
that is how the law, which was meant to ensure man's
happiness, became an end in itself, and the salvation
of man became relegated to a subordinate place.

We might still imagine that Jesus had done away
with the Sabbath in principle, because he adds here:
"The Son of Man is Lord of the sabbath" (Mark 2:28),
a declaration which, in Matthew's version is motivated

by: "Have you not read that the Temple priests break
the sabbath without being blamed for it? Now here,
I tell you, is something more than the Temple" (Matt.
12:5ff.). From the context it is evident that Jesus did
not intend to do away with the Sabbath law. Such
an argument would have been superfluous if He had
wanted to do this. It is clearly a question of the
relative importance of the several laws. In a later day,
when the Sabbath had been replaced by Sunday, the
Church probably added these words from another
part of the text so as to give a reason for the change
in the law. A similar tendency can be found in Luke
(6:5), where a very old manuscript has this addition
to the text: "On the same day, seeing a man working
on the Sabbath day, he said to him: Friend, if you
know what you are doing, (that is to say, if you know
that the Sabbath has been abolished) then I wish you
luck, but if you do not know it, then you are accursed
as a breaker of the law." There can be no doubt
about the later origin of these words, because in the
time of Jesus, no one would have dared to work on
the Sabbath in that way. Emendations of this kind
appear in the Gospels more often than anyone who
is not an expert in biblical exegesis could imagine.
The Church took great liberties in applying the Word
of the Lord: "Whoever hears you, hears me."

Another area in which Jesus repeatedly came into
conflict with the traditional interpretation of the law
was in the case of dietary laws. In this connection
we find the oft-repeated rebuke, "He eats with tax
collectors and sinners." Such people could not help

being ritually unclean, and therefore they could not
have been particularly careful about keeping the
laws of purification. The most elaborate saying about
this question is Mark 7:1-23, a passage which is of the
greatest interest as an illustration of the development
of Christian thought. Mark describes the contents of
these laws in great detail for the benefit of his pagan
readers. (He evidently did not realize, by the way,
that they had originally applied only to the priests.)
Here Jesus does not do away with the law, either,
but only restores the original hierarchy of the laws.
"How ingeniously you get round the commandment
of God in order to preserve your own tradition!"
(Mark 7:9). Jesus does not overthrow the tradition of
the fathers (Matt. 23:2), but he registers a protest
against the practice of putting them on the same
plane with the commandments of God,[6] because, when
they do this, men put the creation of their own hands
above the law of God. So they put external ritual
purity above the purity of the heart which God demands of man[7] (Mark 7:15). The evangelist adds a
conclusion here, also, which reaches much further
than what Jesus intends, and which reflects later
practice: "Thus he pronounced all foods clean" (Mark
7:19).

It will be worth our while to follow the story of
this passage still further, because, as we have already
noted, it illustrates the way in which later tradition
worked. We read in Mark that when they got home,
the disciples asked Jesus the meaning of the parable.
This is a characteristic Marcan twist. Jesus taught

the disciples separately and secretly. But there is no question of a parable here. It is a question of a purely historical fact in the life of Jesus. When such a fact has lost its contemporaneity, then people allegorize it and turn it into a parable. We can see the start of this process in the seven "woes" against the scribes and Pharisees in Matthew. There it says, "You who clean the outside of the cup and dish and leave the inside full of extortion and intemperance . . ." (Matt. 23:25). It is perfectly obvious that the Pharisees didn't wash only the outside of their pottery. Cups and saucers have become images of people here, people who are full of unrighteousness inside. But in Luke the process has gone even further: "You clean the outside of cup and plate, while inside yourselves you are filled with extortion and wickedness" (Luke 11:39). And even more remarkable, to be sure, is what Luke adds to that: "Instead give alms from what is within, and then indeed everything will be clean for you." Luke had a special interest in almsgiving because, during his apostolic voyages with Paul, he was often dependent upon the generosity of the Christian community. But there is even more to the story. The later Latin translation turns this last phrase into "Give whatever is left over as alms." Evidently people found that Luke's recommendation could not be carried out in practice, and changed the text to conform to the practice. This is just a schoolboy's example of the devious ways in which the later Church dealt with the Word of the Lord with a view to maintaining it in drastically altered circumstances. Against this background our earlier assertion that the

Church invested Jesus' casual words with universally valid applications is no longer so shocking.

We could find a great many more examples to show that Jesus broke the Sabbath, not for reasons of necessity, but solely because the commandment of love is the most important one. This is evident from the many healings He performed on the Sabbath. We are not the first ones to point out that the lame man of Bethesda had been sick for thirty-eight years (John 5:5), so that he could very well have waited another few hours. As we have already mentioned, this distinction that Jesus makes between the various laws is a new one. For the Jew all laws come from God and are therefore of equal importance. When the lawyer puts the question, "Which is the greatest commandment?" it is not a question of a practical norm, but of a theoretical conundrum: What is the commandment from which the others can be deduced logically? The author of St. Matthew's Gospel, a lawyer himself, therefore alters Jesus' answer: "There is no commandment greater than these" (Mark 12:31) becomes: "On these two commandments hang the whole Law, and the Prophets also" (Matt. 22:40). Jesus transforms the speculative question into a practical one. How should a person behave in a situation of conflict? Which law has the pre-eminence in such a case? The parable of the Good Samaritan, which in Luke 10:25-37 is attached to this question, makes this clear. The scribe who asks Jesus the question does his best to keep it on a theoretical level, and to that end he asks a second question, one which had also been the subject of endless disputation:

"Who is my neighbour?" Here, too, Jesus at once applies the question to the problem of a practical standard of conduct. You must decide who your neighbor is, and therefore who has the first call on your help, not by putting yourself in the center but by trying to put yourself in the other person's place. The person who is in the greatest need, he is your neighbor, no matter whether he is a Jew or not, no matter whether he is related to you or not.

We are used to thinking of the priest and the Levite who passed by without helping as merciless people, but that is not necessarily correct. Here, too, it is a question of people who are bogged down in their own concept of law. According to the jurispru- dence of the scribes, a law that is certain always takes precedence over a law that is doubtful. Now, it wasn't certain whether or not the man lying there in the road was still alive. The priest and the Levite could not examine him to see if he was still alive because, if he were dead, then they would be ritually unclean (Lev. 21:1). In fact one would already be contaminated if he came within eight feet of the dead person. No, they could not even poke him with a stick to find out if he were still alive, because the law says that contamination is conducted by a stick as big around as the spur of an ox herd.[8]

So, it was not certain that the man was dead, and there was no way of making certain. It was perfectly obvious that he was not a near relative whom one would be obliged to help (according to Lev. 21:22), and that was the only other relevant question. So

they obeyed the commandment which was undoubt-
edly applicable, following the accepted standard that
in case of doubt it is not the importance of the law,
but the degree of certainty, which counts. We must
not forget that they had a lot to lose if they became
contaminated. They would have to go through ritual
purification, an expensive process (Num. 19:1-10). As
long as they remained unclean, they and their families
were not permitted to make use of the income of the
tithes. So they preferred to regard the man as a
dead man, and by doing so would have killed him
by failing to help him. The Samaritan, in contrast,
is a sinful man. He does not have any purity to lose.
He has no credit balance in his spiritual bank account.
Not a thing! But just because of this, he is free with
respect to his neighbor, free to grasp the opportunity
of the moment. And that is precisely the freedom
which Jesus comes to bring to men. God accepts man
in his sinfulness, with all his human shortcomings,
because He is a father who knows how things go
with man. He is the Good Shepherd who ventures
forth to seek the one sheep that is lost. He allows
the weeds to grow up along with the grain, and he
does not judge before the time. Jesus is the prophet,
as we said in the third chapter, and that means that
His entire being is in the image of the invisible God.
He sends the adulterous woman away: "Has no one
condemned you? Then I do not condemn you either."

Someone who knows that a certain person accepts
him feels that he is free when he is with that person.
He knows that he can be himself. He does not always

have to go about on tiptoe, he does not have to wear a mask. In his relations with this person who loves him, he is freed also from the need to show off, a need which is one of the things that makes us so unfree. Because he feels that the love of the other person is free, he does not have to force it by fussing about. Naturally, he will feel obligated to do his best not to disappoint the other person, and to conform to the ideal picture the other person has of him. Therefore Jesus can say to the adulterous woman, "Go, and sin no more." But this is the reply of man to God's freely given love, which frees him from all necessity of showing off before Him.

Thus Jesus of Nazareth did not do away with the law, nor did He even soften it. On the contrary, He restored the law to its full power. "You have learnt how it was said to our ancestors: You must not kill; and if anyone does kill he must answer for it before the court. But I say this to you: anyone who is angry with his brother will answer for it before the court . . ." (Matt. 5:21-22; cf. 5:27, 31, 33). Neither does he act like a psychologist who tries to correct the unconditional and therefore unpsychological character of the law by taking the human situation into consideration as one of the determining factors. No, the paradoxical thing about Jesus' teaching is precisely that He brings the law into its fullest scope, and yet does not minimize human capabilities in any way. The biblical image of creation out of nothing is the expression of a belief in the original integrity and unity of man. Jesus is himself such a perfect man, brought forth in purity from the creating hands of God. Nowhere in His words do we find any complaint about man's moral weakness, any reference to the fact that man does the things he really does not want to do, and that he is unable to accomplish the good things he really wants to do. Jesus is no Paul, no Augustine, no Luther.

For Jesus, the meaning of the law is, more than anything else, an indicator of the ideal which will set a person in the right direction, which, to tell the truth, was the original meaning of the word **torah** (see the first chapter). Thus, when He is asked to make a juridical decision, He refuses categorically: "My friend . . . who appointed me your judge, or the arbitrator of your claims? (Luke 12:14). Also, He doesn't want to be called Rabbi (Matt. 23:7).[9] He does not teach, he preaches. That is to say, He does not set down carefully weighed rules of conduct; rather, He preaches an ideal: "You must therefore be perfect just as your heavenly Father is perfect" (Matt. 5:48). The danger of every rule of conduct is that people mistake this minimum requirement for an absolute norm of moral behavior. Therefore, Jesus is not satisfied with setting down norms. He presents an ideal. And the purpose of this ideal is not that of bringing us to a "salutary doubt," as Luther taught.[10] Such a Pauline concept is foreign to Jesus. Oh, yes, He knows the cleavage between the radical demands of the law and the weakness of man, but for Jesus that weakness is the starting point, and man does not have to be brought to a state of doubt by confrontation with a law which he cannot live up to.

Thus Jesus is able to gather up His teaching into the mighty saying, "Do not imagine that I have come to abolish the Law or the Prophets. I have come not to abolish but to complete them. I tell you solemnly, till heaven and earth disappear, not one dot, not one little stroke, shall disappear from the Law until its purpose is achieved" (Matt. 5:17-18). This saying has been called the most Jewish of all the texts of the New Testament, and many scholars do not believe it is authentic.[11] According to them, this saying came into being in reaction against a development within the Gentile Christian group in the Church which Paul organized. The old Jewish core of Christians regarded this development with anxious concern, and attempted by means of this saying to erect a bulwark against a creeping libertinism within the Hellenistic community. Thus they set the clock back, and the royal freedom which Jesus had preached was in part swept aside in order to make room for a Jewish-Christian legal ethic. I myself believe that the development was rather the reverse and that the following verses, which express a more liberal attitude toward the law "the man who infringes even one of the least of these commandments . . . will be considered the least in the kingdom of heaven" [Matt. 5:19], are an addition of the later Church. Luke is, after all, writing for Gentile Christian readers, and the fact that he puts this saying in a rather special context (16:7) is reason for reflection. Elsewhere Luke has no compunctions about omitting mention of the setting if it seems more useful to him. The introductory phrase "I tell you solemnly" is normally taken to be the hallmark of an authentic saying of Jesus.[12] But the fact that the expression "a jot or a tittle of law" can also be found in Jewish literature is not conclusive evidence that the saying is of Jewish origin. The negative form which the saying takes here makes it clear that a debate is going on. Someone is rebuking Jesus for breaking the law, and He replies with a statement that is familiar to them because it comes from their own legal writings. We see the same technique used in the question about the greatest commandment (Mark 12:28-34), where Jesus replies by putting these two commandments in juxtaposition, just as the Jews themselves had done.[13]

Thus, as we have said, the development went in the opposite direction. Jesus himself upheld the law in its original strength. "In the beginning it was not so . . ." (Matt. 19:8). For Him the law is the expression of the will of His Father, which is daily bread for Him (John 30:34). He has fulfilled the law down to its most minute details, even to wearing the prescribed fringes on His garments (Mark 6:56; Luke 8:34). But he does not **merely** fulfill the law. He elevates the fulfilling of the law to a higher plane. In this sense, too, He can say that He has come to fulfill the law. To him, fulfillment of the law is the expression of His love for the Father: "If you love me, you will keep my commandments . . ." (John 14:15). Where there is love, there the law is experienced no longer as law but as freedom. It is Paul who has thought this idea through with especial care, and for that reason the final chapter of this work is devoted to him.

An important question still remains for us to

answer. If it is the case that in His teaching and in His life Jesus preached the true fulfillment of the Mosaic law, how then is it possible for the early Church, with an uninhibitedness which it was never able to recapture in later ages, to do away with the greater part of the law of Moses in a few years? The simplest solution would lie in the assumption that Jesus did not want to do away with the law himself, but left the task to His disciples. We might even quote Matthew 5:19; in support of this contention. We should have to paraphrase the text in some such way as this: "In due time, circumstances may well make it necessary for you to do away with one or another of these laws, but you must not imagine that you are going to get a fine place in heaven as a reward for doing this. On the contrary, the person who remains faithful to the law, because, in spite of all its imperfections it remains the translation into human terms of God's will, that person is great before God." This saying would then have come from another context originally, namely, the instruction of the disciples, and Matthew would have placed it with the saying about the jot and tittle, in keeping with his habit of stringing together texts that are related in content. Nor does it seem impossible to believe that it is this saying, and not the preceding one, which was created by the later Church in order to justify a practice which had already grown up, just as was done in the case of the Sabbath and the dietary laws.

At the same time, there are other elements in the life and teaching of Jesus to which we can point,

from which the Church derived the conviction that
by doing away with the Jewish law she was fulfilling
the will of her divine Master. Pre-eminent among
these is the aura of sovereign freedom which con-
tinues to surround Jesus, despite all His faithfulness
to the Jewish law. And this is because the law is to
Him the will of His heavenly Father, whom He
always addresses devotedly as "Abba," Father (which
sounded much the way "Papa" sounds to us). The
law is the law of His heavenly Father, so it is impossible for it to be inhuman, and if the Church then
went on to refuse to make the law binding upon the
Gentiles, it was precisely because the law marred
the image of the heavenly Father for these people.

The distinction which Jesus made between one
law and another certainly helped this process along.
The great emphasis He put on the law of Love
deprived the ceremonial laws of much of their importance, and they therefore fell by the wayside. It
is understandable that to justify this, cases where
Jesus permitted the law of Love to prevail over a
Sabbath or dietary law were used as examples. Still,
this does not explain everything. In the first place,
the examples may simply have been justifications
after the fact, and besides, much more important laws,
such as the law of circumcision, were abandoned
without any attempt being made to justify this by
finding examples in the life of Jesus.

It is my feeling that only one possible answer is
left, and this answer is so simple that it is almost
simplistic. The Church saw the hand of God in the

fact that it was impossible to bring the heathen under
the Jewish law. Again and again we see how sensitive
the young Church is to the activity of God in history.
The diaconate originates in a trivial women's quarrel.
The conversion of Europe probably occurred thanks
to a rather ordinary setback of Paul's. "Having been
told by the Holy Spirit not to preach the word in
Asia . . ." is the way Luke puts it (Acts 16:6), and
further on he writes that the Spirit of Jesus did not
allow them to journey to Bithynia. Was it a bridge
that had washed away, or a missed connection between caravans? We don't know; but the apostles
were convinced that the Spirit was leading them,
just as Jesus had been driven by the Spirit.

This condition of surrender to the will of God can
be attributed to a special charism with which the
apostles, as founders of the Church, were endowed.
But it is better to suppose that they had gained from
their Master the deep humility which is the hallmark
of the man who knows that He should wait upon God.
When St. Paul says that Christ humbled himself to
death on the cross (Phil. 2:8), he is not merely referring to the humiliating character of death by
crucifixion, the most scandalous death imaginable in
his time. There is no doubt that he also means to
indicate that Jesus was obedient to the facts and to
the people who bore down upon Him in life. There
was no voice from heaven which revealed to Him
that He must die a hero's death. It was the pitiable
passion of men, the jealousy of the priests, envy,
political intrigue, and other such subtleties which

brought Him to the cross. But in the darkness of His abandonment by God on the cross He found God's presence, and that is His real greatness.

6

"... YOU ARE [NO LONGER]

UNDER LAW . . ."

ROMANS 6:14, RSV

Paul is the apostle of Christian freedom. The statistics of the vocabulary of the New Testament show us this without the need of any additional proof. The noun "freedom" is found nowhere but in Paul's writings, where it appears seven times. The adjective "free" appears sixteen times in Paul, and only seven times elsewhere. The verb "to free" is used five times by Paul, and only twice by others. The atmosphere of his letters speaks more eloquently than these dry numbers. Wherever one turns in the writings of Paul, one is fascinated again and again by the fact of coming face to face with a man who is convinced that he is free: free from everything that lies behind him, who feels that he is a new man; even that he is a new creature (Eph. 4:24; Col. 3:10; 2 Cor. 5:17; Gal. 6:15). "It is the same God that said, 'Let there be light shining out of darkness' who has shone in our minds to radiate the light of the knowledge of God's glory, the glory on the face of Christ" (2 Cor. 4:6). It is an impression no one can escape if he has occupied himself even a little with Paul's writings. But what is the basis for this feeling which permeates the apostle's life? For us this is a question that is vastly more important than merely establishing the fact, and it is a question that is not at all easy to answer. Here the words of Peter, in the second Epistle, come to our rescue: "Our brother Paul, who is so dear to us, told you this when he wrote you with the wisdom which is his special gift. He always writes like this when he deals with this sort of subject, and this makes points in his letter hard to understand . . ." (2 Pet. 3:15-16). We should not be too surprised by this. St. Paul is really the first Christian theologian, and he has therefore to find his way in an entirely unexplored country. We must bear in mind also that he is actually a busy missionary, and only occasionally gets a chance to put his ideas into writing. Furthermore, we are dealing here with a question which always remains to a large extent a mystery, because the meeting of God with man always occurs in a shadow of mystery, and words always fall short in describing it. We are definitely dealing with that kind of meeting here, because freedom comes from God, while laws are things that man has made.

Of Paul even more than of Jesus, it is said that he did away with the law of Moses. It was someone no less distinguished than the great Roman Catholic exegete Lagrange who said in his majestic commentary on the Epistle to the Romans that the real service of Paul is that he proclaimed the doing away with the law for Jews as well as for the heathen, and that everyone agreed about this.[1] Before we test Lagrange's categorical statement against the facts, we should focus our attention on one fact that we do not think can be disputed, a fact which must be the starting point for any further discussion. If Paul did away with the law, then he did so with the help of the law itself, specifically by showing that the law itself bears witness to its temporary nature, and that its actual meaning is not what it at first sight seems to be. Even a superficial acquaintance with the Letters of Paul enables us to know how important a place Old Testament proof texts have in them. Is it possible to accuse Paul of the unparalleled enormity of basing his message on Scripture, but at the same time simply abandoning the law of Moses, which is the heart of that Scripture?

Now we find a certain way of using proof texts in later writers, and specially in the Church Fathers (by the way, this is proof of how serious the problem still was at that time), which we do not find in Paul.

It is true that we find traces of an allegorical understanding of Scripture in him, as in 1 Corinthians 9:9, where the command which forbids muzzling the ox that treads out the grain (Deut. 25:4) is applied to the preacher, and his right to make a living by preaching. He is saying that it is always clear that God is really talking about people rather than about animals. But turns of thought like this appear only sporadically, and besides, there is a real likelihood that Paul is simply trying to be witty here.

Even if one assumes that Paul did away with the law of Moses, it is clear that he put in its place a set of prescriptions for the Christian life that is no less detailed. So this much-touted Christian freedom might still seem to be nothing more than a farce. One thinks immediately of the requirement that a woman may not take part in the worship of God without having her head covered (1 Cor. 11:1-16), a regulation that until very recently has been taken so seriously in the Roman Catholic Church that women have been kept out of church for not having a hat on. And in Muslim countries, where it is a grave discourtesy for a man to go bareheaded in the presence of his superiors, men were forced to enter church without their headdress. And this is just something that got into a letter by accident, and which was preserved only through still further accidents. Just imagine what a lot of rules Paul must have given verbally. When one thinks of it, what a blessing that Paul did not write everything down. Never mind, it is perfectly obvious from this that Paul was no antinomian, and when he says that the Christian is no longer under the law (Rom. 6:14; Gal. 5:18) he cannot mean that the law of Moses is done away with, because he could immediately have been accused of driving out the devil with Beelzebub. There's absolutely no excuse for the Christian theologian to speak disparagingly of the Jewish law with its 610 ordinances, and never open his mouth about the codex of Church law with its 2,414 canons.

There is another misinterpretation closely allied to this, and one comes across it again and again in Christian writers. It is to the effect that Paul was

weighed down by the oppressive burden of the
Jewish law, which he was not able to fulfill, and that
Christian freedom consisted in the fact that the New
Law gave, along with its commandments, the strength
to carry them out. The initial presupposition is not
correct. The Pharisees, Paul among them, did not in
the least have the impression that they could not
carry out the requirements of the law. Quite the
contrary. They were convinced that they obeyed the
law unfailingly. To be sure, they realized that they
fell short of the mark occasionally, but the law itself
gave them the means to make up for these shortcomings by sacrifices and free-will offerings. That
Paul shared this confidence in the possibility of keeping the law we can see from his own testimony: "As
far as the law can make you perfect, I was faultless"
(Phil. 3:6; Gal. 1:14) What he gave up when he was
converted was not a heavy burden, but something
profitable (Phil. 13:7). When Peter said, at the so-
called Apostolic Council, that the law is an intolerable
burden (Acts 15:10), and when Jesus says that His
teaching is an easy burden in comparison with that
of the scribes (Matt. 11:30), they are referring to the
difficulties of the simple, uneducated man, who does
not know the law, and who has no way of learning it,
and whose activities continually keep him impure, so
that he has always to be reckoned in the caste of the
untouchables. The Pharisees had arranged for themselves all the loopholes they needed to enable them to
escape from the requirements of ritual purity. Jesus is
not being unfair when He condemns them: "They tie
up heavy burdens and lay them on men's shoulders,

but will they lift a finger to move them? Not they!"
(Matt. 23:4). They shut other men out of the kingdom
of heaven, and at the same time they fail to go in
themselves (Matt. 23:13). The apocryphal Gospel of
Thomas puts it even more vividly, in a saying that
may well be from Jesus himself: "They are like a
dog who sleeps in the manger, who does not eat the
fodder himself, but who prevents the oxen from eating
it" (Gospel of Thomas, 102).

The conversion of Paul, then, is not a moral re-
direction, like that of Augustine. Still less is it the
result of a spiritual crisis, as Luther's was. The word
"conversion" (**metanoia**) seldom appears in his Epis-
tles, certainly much less often than it does in the
Gospels. Near Damascus the mysteries of Christ,
previously hidden in the Scriptures, are revealed to
Paul (Eph. 3:2-7), specifically, the fact that the
heathen has been called. Thus his conversion is
really more truly a call to be an apostle to the
Gentiles, as he himself tells us (Gal. 1:15). Still
better, he was born an apostle, but now suddenly he
sees that he has been proclaiming the wrong message.

The mistaken supposition we have been speaking
about is based primarily on a much misunderstood
passage from the Epistle to the Romans (7:14-24) with
its celebrated exclamation, the one Augustine made
his very own, "Every single time. I want to do good,
it is something evil that comes to hand" (Rom. 7:21).
Here Paul is speaking about his own past, and about
the Pharisee in general, but he is doing it in the light
of a Christian insight which he acquired later on. In

his eyes, the Pharisee is a man who is arrogant to the very depths of his being, to such an extent that even his good deeds are perverted, so he does evil at the very moment he is trying to do good.

But the second part of our introductory statement is also false: the notion that the new law is a well-spring of strength which puts man into a condition in which he can fulfill the law. None of us experiences this. Paul does say time and time again that the old law gives no strength, and that it leads all the more quickly to sin because, being a challenge, it makes the evil more conscious (Rom. 7:7; 5:20). But it still does not follow from this that the new law gives strength. The very expression "new law" is unknown to Paul. The introductory statement depended on agreeing with St. Thomas Aquinas' belief that "new law" means grace.[2] But then we have no right to deny grace to the Old Testament man.

So we come to the conclusion that Paul did not do away with the law of Moses. He is not aware of the existence of an old law and a new law. There is only one law, and that is the law of God, which is also the law of Christ (1 Cor. 9:21; Gal. 6:2). When he says that the whole of the law is summed up in the single commandment of love (Rom. 13:8-10; Gal. 5:14), he certainly implies that the Christian must fulfill the entire law. Otherwise, what would be the purpose of the remark? To be sure, this law is not rigid and immovable. No, it was not like that for the Jew to begin with. And we can also say with confidence that preaching to the Gentiles, in which

Paul was the great pioneer, required radical adaptation. But at the same time it remained in principle the same law, just as the New Israel, the Church, is in principle the continuation of the old people of God, like a new branch grafted onto an old stem (Rom. 11:16-24).

The modifications and adaptations did not apply to converts from Judaism. They had to remain true to the law of Moses, just as Paul himself did. On his final visit to Jerusalem, he was challenged to demonstrate this by paying a so-called purification offering on behalf of the less-well-off Jewish Christians. "This will let everyone know that there is no truth in the reports that they have heard about you, and that you still regularly observe the Law" (Acts 21:24). Paul took up the challenge without hesitation, which certainly showed that he wanted to be taken for a Jew who was faithful to the law.

On the other side, even with these modifications, the law was certainly not a liberating instrument for the converts from paganism, who were accustomed to a far more lax moral standard. Paul had good reason to tell the Corinthian believers that "people of immoral lives, idolaters, adulterers, calamites, sodomites, thieves, usurers, drunkards, slanderers, and swindlers will never inherit the kingdom of God" (1 Cor. 6:10; cf. Gal. 5:19-21; 1 Tim. 1:10). Thus it is difficult to see how the preaching of Christian duty, even if this were limited to the Ten Commandments, could have seemed to involve a liberation in what concerned morality.

As if the problem were not difficult enough already, we encounter people in the Letters of Paul who will not accept the fact that the Jewish law no longer has any force for them, and who get themselves circumcised, observe various festivals, keep the dietary laws, and so on. In his Letters to the congregations of Asia Minor, that is, Galatians and Colossians, Paul has the greatest difficulty in keeping his new converts from just this sort of thing. "It is I, Paul, who tell you this, if you allow yourselves to be circumcised, Christ will be of no benefit to you at all. With all solemnity I repeat my warning: everyone who accepts circumcision is obliged to keep the whole Law. But if you do look to the Law to make you justified, then you have separated yourself from Christ, and have fallen from grace" (Gal. 5:2-4). "From now onwards, never let anyone else decide what you should eat or drink, or whether you are to observe annual festivals, New Moons, or sabbaths" (Col. 2:16). Must we gather from this that Paul wants to force on his converts a freedom they have not asked for, in somewhat the same way as in our own time certain modernists among the clergy insist on talking about all kinds of freedom to believers who care nothing about them? Is that not destroying freedom in the name of freedom?

It is clearly a question here of people who find the Christian faith rather sober, and who want to take on certain Jewish customs as a matter of devotion. They want to be more Roman than the Pope. But what is so dreadful is that Paul has to write

such a violent letter about it, in which he speaks of
"garbage" and of "another gospel" (Gal. 1:6). He
reminds them again of the labor pains of Christian
rebirth (Gal. 4:19), and tells them that he fears he has
wasted his time worrying himself to death about them
(Gal. 4:11). "Stand firm," he cries (Gal. 5:1), and that
is something he says only at moments of ultimate
peril.

If we are going to understand this, we shall have
to see it against the background of Paul's own life.
As we explained in the fourth chapter, the gracious
character of the Covenant became obscured in later
Judaism, and it degenerated into a contract between
two parties of equal dignity. For this reason the God
of love was demoted to a bookkeeper who had only
to total up a set of figures when one's life was over.
Jewish writers criticize Paul for putting things too
much into absolutes of black and white, as well as
for letting his own past experience color his ideas
too deeply. But one can find a turn of mind even in
the Jewish literature of today which is not so different
from this. Thus Mendele Moicher Sforim (S. J.
Abramowitsj) writes: "When a Jew has told God his
tale of woe, and has sung a hymn to Him, he is
confident that he has done everything that lies in his
power. He is at peace, and as happy as a child who,
after he has been beaten, wipes his tears away and
is quiet. I sit down in peace on the driver's box of
my wagon, stroke my beard contentedly, as if I would
say, "Lord of the world, I have done my part. Now it
is your turn.' "³ Whatever else there is to be said,

Paul believed that he had gravely misused God's
condescending goodness, and that he had treated the
Covenant as a means by which he could raise himself
to God's own level.

At the pinnacle of his accomplishment, when he
was still trying to bring others to faithfulness to the
law by the use of force, God grasped Paul, and told
him that he was fighting on the wrong side; that
Jesus of Nazareth—who promised forgiveness to tax
collectors and sinners, thereby making the whole
system of laws count for nothing—was the Messiah
whom God had promied. This occurrence determined
Paul's spirituality for the rest of his life. Whenever
anyone is tempted to take pride in himself or in his
own power, he finds Paul dead set against him.
Whether it is pride in faithfulness to the law, like the
pride Paul himself once had, and which he describes
under the name of "Judaism" in the Epistle to the
Romans, or if it is pride in human knowledge, as it
was in Corinth, or in one or another devotional
practice, as it was in Galatia or Colossae, it is all the
same to Paul: it is treason against the cross of Christ,
the cross, which conclusively put an end to all human
pride (Gal. 5:11).

As soon as a person starts to take pride in himself,
and looks to his own strength for salvation, he forfeits
not only grace, but Christian freedom as well (Gal.
5:4). For Paul, freedom consists in the fact, not that
a man can dispose of himself, but that a man places
himself at the disposal of God. As soon as man
desires to dispose of himself he lives under the pres-

sure of having to exert himself, and it is precisely this which makes him unfree. Human craving to be worthy is what Paul calls "the flesh." It is the greatest possible threat to freedom. A person feels and knows that his worth consists in the value put on him by others, or by the Other. A person who lives utterly alone on an otherwise uninhabited island cannot feel that he is valuable. Unless someone evaluates us or our work, we feel worthless. It is not possible simply to be good or righteous. We are these things only in relation to someone, just as our whole existence is an "I-thou" relationship. As a result, men have an irresistible urge to mean something to someone else, and to be of value. But we know also that the appreciation and love of others is not given against their will. Love and appreciation can be given only in freedom. God cannot be forced, either. No, especially not God! All we can do is to let Him take possession of us in grace. This is how grace makes men free; it liberates them from the debilitating compulsion of trying to amount to something in comparison with God. And in this way it becomes understandable that Paul sets grace over against law in absolute contrast (Rom. 6:14). And law here means the entire system (every conceivable system) of salvation by means of laws.

Perhaps it seems strange that Paul is still able to speak of being "called to freedom" (Gal. 5:13) and of the obedience of faith (Rom. 1:5; 16:26). Will not everyone receive this message of grace and liberation gladly? If we think about this at all, we will discover that it is extremely difficult for anyone to give himself unconditionally to someone else. We want always to be doing something for the other person, so as to make ourselves indispensable, and to bind the other person to us so we can exact an earnest of his love and loyalty. And here is just the place where we lose out on love. Naturally, this does not mean we ought to sit idly by with our hands in our pockets, let alone that we ought to sin so as to make God's grace flow more plentifully. St. Paul was told that his spirituality led necessarily to this conclusion (Rom. 3:5; 6:1). But the conclusion is not a correct one. Paul never boasts of his sins. He does not have the unhealthy inclination to be an "honest to God" sinner. On the contrary, he feels he has been grasped by Christ (Phil. 3:12), and as a result he is always grasping after perfection. But he does not do this in order to conquer Christ; he does it because Christ has conquered him.

And so, grace makes him a new man, a new creature, for love has a creative power. We all know that love and friendship change people, that they change people so profoundly that even strangers can see they have become different people. Just because love has taken him for a better man than he is, a man will try to answer to this ideal image, not in an effort to become worthy of the love, but because someone else's valuation has indeed made him into a different person.

Love like this also frees a man from his past shortcomings. Not that the facts can be put out of existence. What has gone before even God himself cannot undo. But, because He approaches me just as I am, with my sins and my weaknesses, He liberates me from this sinful past, and makes me new from day to day (2 Cor. 4:16). He cloaks our sinful footsteps behind us with the mantle of His love, and teaches us not to look back (Phil. 3:13).

In conclusion, the loving response of man also frees him from the law, in the sense that there no longer is any law for him. Therefore Paul can say, "If you are led by the Spirit, no law can touch you" (Gal. 5:18). This spirit is the love of God, poured into our hearts (Rom. 5:5). Not that love can actually take the place of a commandment, but that living with God quite naturally gives a person a sort of instinct by means of which he senses intuitively what God requires of him in a given situation—somewhat as the body "automatically" picks up the things that have nutritional value, and rejects those parts of its food which are harmful. But for all their love, the Corinthian believers had a certain amount of difficulty discovering that a woman must not appear with her head uncovered during the worship of God. Once and for all, laws are indispensable when people have to live together. We may even suppose that as society becomes increasingly complicated, the "traffic laws" have to become more and more complicated. Many areas of life used to be unstructured: road traffic, social security, hygiene, and so on. And our present-day structures may soon extend to areas we used to consider to be inalienably personal. Consider com-

pulsory education, for instance, or innoculation, fluori-
dation, and so on. Who can tell how much further
this will go in the future? Perhaps obligatory medical
examination before marriage will soon be a matter
of law.

Teilhard de Chardin tells us that this increasing
complexity must be compensated for by a stronger
interiority, a binding principle. And that is love, the
"bond of perfection" (Col. 3:14).

But when all is said and done, it remains true that
there is a certain kind of proliferation of laws which
tends to obscure the image of our merciful Father.
"The spirit of freedom can with difficulty accompany
the multiplication of ecclesiastical laws," said Monsignor Arceo-Méndez at the Second Vatican Council
(October 27, 1964). If you truly love, you will easily,
even gladly, do what the Other asks of you. The
girl who is in love will gladly prepare her fiancé's
favorite dish. But if he writes out a menu for the
entire week, it may put their love in jeopardy.

One more observation to conclude: It is often said
that the redeemed Christian frequently looks unsaved.
Karl Rahner once remarked that it was no wonder
modern man had so little interest in grace and
salvation, when theologians always insisted on referring their effects to the realm of pure metaphysics.
It is very difficult to get excited about something that
no one can possibly notice.[4] And Fortmann adds:
"When Scripture speaks with so much emphasis about
freedom in the Holy Spirit, for example, is it not

obvious that it is speaking about something tangible, something that can be experienced? If freedom is the hallmark of redeemed existence, then there must be evidences of it somewhere."⁵ Does this not happen because our teaching about salvation is so completely juridical? It is an article of faith that Christ died for us all, and that by this we are saved. But this remains a cold doctrine and we have a lot of trouble getting enthused about it: God demands satisfaction for our sins from His Son. Can one call that a message of liberation, a gospel of freedom?

Possibly we should say that Paul himself is responsible for the existence of this image (for to speak of "salvation" is to speak in imagery, though we often forget it). Some quotations: "Christ redeemed us from the curse of the Law by being cursed for our sake, since the scripture says: **Cursed be everyone who is hanged on a tree**" (Gal. 3:13). This is not exactly the clearest of reasoning. And it is even more difficult to follow the apostle in his allegory of marriage in Romans 7:1-3. A married woman is bound to her husband, but as soon as he dies, she is free, and in this sense at least, she is no longer under the law. "That is why you, my brothers, who through the body of Christ are now dead to the Law, can now give yourselves to another husband, to him who rose from the dead . . ." (Rom. 7:4). The theological contortions into which the apostle has to force himself here show that this cannot be the heart of his message of liberation. The heart of the gospel, the Good News, is the message of forgiveness that Jesus preached. For that message He not only risked His life, but forfeited it. But God raised Him from the dead to show that He was right, and to place the seal of His own faithfulness on the message of Jesus. But the message does not begin with the cross. The cross is an enigma, the positive value of which Jesus discovered only gradually, as witness His prayer, "Father, if it be possible, let this cup pass from me." But at his very birth the name "Jesus" was given to him, the name which means God has saved His people (Matt. 1:21), and His entire life is a demonstration of the mercy of the heavenly Father who sympathizes with the misery of mankind.

But for Paul, the Jew, it remains a painful enigma that the Son of God, the promised Messiah, is nailed to the cross. In its effort to make the enigma somewhat palatable to the Jews of that time, the Church from the very outset referred to the Scriptures: it had to be this way. And that is why St. Paul's theory about the saving power of the cross gives such a strong impression of artificiality. He is in the last analysis attempting to explain something which ultimately is and shall always remain a mystery, just as all suffering is a mystery. But that is not the Good News. The liberating Word of Jesus Christ is this: God has inscribed our sins in the sand, but our names in the palm of His hand.

NOTES

1. "The Truth Will Make You Free"
   1. G. Marcel, **Being and Having** (New York: Harper & Row).
   2. A. Gide, **Immoralist** (New York: Vintage Books).
   3. J. P. Sartre, **Nausea** (New York: New Directions).
   4. R. C. Kwant, **Encounter** (Pittsburgh: Duquesne University Press).
   5. W. Luypen, **Existential Phenomenology** (**Aula** 68), (Utrecht/Antwerpen ²1961), p. 191.
   6. H. Thielicke, **The Individual and the System.**
   7. J. P. Sartre, **The Devil and the Good Lord and Two Other plays** (New York: Knopf, 1960).
   8. Citation from: **Humanus** (J. H. Walgrave), "The Idea of Our Fourfold Freedom, **Kultuurleven** 19 (1952), p. 172.
   9. J. P. Sartre, **No Exit and The Flies** (New York: Knopf, 1947).
   10. R. Bultmann, "The Meaning of the Idea of Freedom for the Occidental Culture," in **Existence and Faith,** II.
   11. R. Bultmann, "The Meaning of God's Word in the New Testament," in **Existence and Faith,** I (New York: Meridian Books).

2. "And Yahweh Spoke to Moses"
   1. See L. Grollenberg, **The Pentateuch** (1965), p. 5.
   2. **Beresjit** I, 1-3.
   3. See E. Jacobs, "Ras Sjamra and The Old Testament" (**Bible and Archeology,** 11), (Nijkerk, 1962), p. 130.
   4. See R. de Vaux, **Ancient Israel: Its Life and Institutions** (New York: McGraw-Hill Book Co., 1961).
   5. Acc. H. Cazelles, **Studies on the Code of Alliance** (Paris, 1946), pp. 133 f.

6. G. Simenon, **The Man with the Little Dog** (from the French).

7. R. Bultmann, **Jesus Christ and Mythology** (New York: Charles Scribner's Sons, 1958).

8. G. Marcel, **op. cit.**

3. ". . . You Build the Sepulchres of the Prophets"

1. A. de Froe/J. Sperna Weiland, **Genesis** (Amsterdam, 1964), p. 27.

2. We discussed this question in detail in the review, **Dux,** 28 (1961), pp. 187-201: "Guilt in Old Testament Perspective." Some parts of this article are used here in a shorter version.

3. "Who has sworn, whether through a sudden fright or through whatever other cause, while he was reading the Scripture or saying a benediction, man will separate him and he will not return in the counsel of the community" (1 QS 7:1).

4. Literally in the Greek text **fysei,** which means "out of nature." I do not know if this was the origin of "Natural Law."

5. See R. Mohr, **Christian Ethics in the Light of Ethnology** (Munich, 1954).

6. H. Renckens, **Israel's Vision on the Past** (The Hague: Tielt, 1956).

7. N. Lohfink, "Law and Grace," in **The Song of Victory at the Sea of Shells** (Frankfurt/Main, 1965), pp. 160 f. See also the article, "Freedom and Repetition," in the same volume.

8. G. Bornkamm, **Jesus of Nazareth** (New York: Harper & Row, 1960).

9. G. Ebeling, **Christian Faith** (from the German).

4. ". . . The Rules and Decrees of the Law"

1. John A. T. Robinson, **Christian Morals Today** (Philadelphia: Westminster Press, 1964).

2. "So many stakes (pales) so many gaps (breaks). G. Bornkamm, **op. cit.** (This typical expression is similar to the English expression: "As many ideas as there are people.")

3. See p. 31.

4. Robinson, op. cit.

5. H. Mulisch, The Affaire 40/61 (Kwadraatpocket 4) (Amsterdam, 1964), p. 166.

6. See M. Noth, "The Laws in Pentateuch," in Collective Studies to the Old Testament.

7. See Masters of Yiddish Story-telling (Amsterdam, ²1964), pp. 23 f.

5. "I Have Come Not to Abolish . . ."

1. L. Cerfaux, The Christian in the Theology of St. Paul (Bilthoven, 1964), p. 11.

2. E. Stauffer, Jesus and His Story (New York: Alfred A. Knopf, 1960), p. 7: "However Jesus is not so much a child of his time and his people as in general was thought, until our time. He is much more lonely, war-like, revolutionary, as man has understood."

3. So, e.g., recently E. Hamel, Natural Law and Law of Christ (Brugge / Paris, 1964), p. 34.

4. Mekhiltha Exodus 31:13; see Strack/Billerbeck, II, 5.

5. See B. Häring, "The Doctrine of Freedom with St. Paul, Ethics of the Law and Ethics of the Situation," in Studiorum Paulinorum Congressus, Vol. I (Rome, 1963), p. 172.

6. Compare with the reply of Rabbi Shammai on this question: "How many Commandments are there? Two, a verbal and a written Torah"; Talmud, Sabbat 31a; Strack/Billerbeck, I, 930.

7. "A lawyer, who knew the Bible very well, and lived in the Baroque-period, thought to find here a Jesuanic prohibition to smoke": E. Stauffer, The Message of Jesus in the Past and Now.

8. Mishna, Toharoth 16, 1.

9. Matt. 13:52 is an oratio pro domo of the author of this Gospel, who seems to be himself a member of the circle of scribes.

10. In the same way modern Lutheran authors also learn. E. Thurneysen compares the reader of the Gospel with a man who stands before a perpendicular wall in the Alps and who is told: "Beyond, the road goes further, a hundred meters higher." E. Thurneysen, **Sermon on the Mount** (Richmond: John Knox, 1964).

11. R. Bultman, **Theology of the New Testament**, 2 vols. (New York: Charles Scribner's Sons). Considering other words of Jesus and considering the real behavior of Jesus, impossible to have an authentic word.

12. A clear example is Mark 9:1: a Word from the Scriptures, the Church did not create herself.

13. See Stauffer, **The Message of Jesus.**

6. ". . . You Are [No Longer] under Law . . ."

1. M. J. Lagrange, **Epistle to the Romans** (Paris, ²1922), p. 180.

2. "Et ideo principaliter lex nova est ipsa gratia Spiritus Sancti," **Summa Theologica**, I-II, q. 106, a. 1. The expression "The new Law" seems to come from Irenaeus (**Adv. Haer.** 4, 34, 4 (**P.G.** 7, 1085C).

3. M. M. Sforim, "Rabbi Mendel Meets Rabbi Alter," in **Masters of the Hebrew Art of Story-telling** (Amsterdam, 1965), p. 16.

4. K. Rahner, **Nature and Grace (Dilemmas in the Modern Church,** II) (New York: Sheed and Ward, 1964).

5. H. M. M. Fortmann, "The Delivering Love," in **The Healing Power of Love** (Utrecht/Antwerpen, 1958), p. 26.